AD VENTURER'S GUIDE
THE
M AGDALEN ISLANDS
TO THE

GEORGE FISCHER

NIMBUS
PUBLISHING

To my sons, Sean and Ryan Fischer.

Nimbus Publishing Limited
P.O. Box 9301, Station A
Halifax, N.S.
B3K 5N5
(902)455-4286

Design: Kathy Kaulbach, Halifax
Printed and bound in Canada

All photos courtesy of George Fischer and the Association Touristique des Iles-de-la-Madeleine.

Canadian Cataloguing in Publication Data
Fischer, George, 1954-
The adventurer's guide to the Magdalen Islands
ISBN 1-55109-088-0
1. Îles-de-la-Madeleine (Quebec)—Guidebooks. 2. Hiking—Quebec—Îles-de-la-Madeleine—Guidebooks. 3. Mountaineering—Quebec—Îles-de-la-Madeleine—Guidebooks. 4.Cycling—Quebec—Îles-de-la-Madeleine—Guidebooks. I. Title.

FC2945.I45A3 1995   917.14′797044   C95-950148-7
F1054.M18F56 1995

Contents

Walking—A Window on Culture

Walking allows us to move through time. It may take a little
longer than mechanized modes of transportation, but it is an
activity that offers a sensory experience. Anyone who has
encountered the wind on the summit of a hill on the Magdalen
Islands will know that walking can lead to a range of discoveries—
of nature and of one's self.

An avid explorer of our time, Wilfrid Thesiger, beautifully
articulates the gifts of walking:

"It often struck me as incredible, especially when I
was travelling on foot and conscious of every one of my foot-
steps, that we could cover such distances by advancing at
such a low speed.... I had no desire however to travel any
faster. Travelling as I did, I had the time to notice a mass
of details: a grasshopper under a bush, a dead swallow on
the ground, the prints of a hare, a bird's nest, the shape and
colour of undulations in the sand, the flowering of tiny
young shoots that push through the soil. I had the time to
pick a plant, to observe a rock. The very slowness of walking alleviates monotony. I imagined how tedious it would be
to cross this same region at high speed in an automobile."

Walking in the Magdalen Islands, a small archipelago scarcely
80 kilometres long, is a comparable experience. It is perhaps the
best way to peer into the nature of island life: the enticing sea,
the steady wind, the sloping dunes, the insular islands, the traditional dwellings. In an island setting, delicacy and roughness, the
minute and the gigantic, occur in proximity—as do scarcity and
abundance, noise and silence. Such contrasts soften, though, in
the temporary hues of daylight turning to dusk.

Following the walking itineraries in this book, you will see
birds common or rare, you may encounter a fisherman in port, or
a family picking wild strawberries in the early morning, or a
child practising his swimming lessons amid the waves of the vast
sea. And because in the Magdalen Islands the seashore is always
close by, you will witness time and again the contrasts between
land and sea. The coast is also a place of perpetual human
exchanges that are carried out sometimes amid a whispering
calm, at other times amid the racket of a nearby public market.

This guidebook by George Fischer will help you plan your out-
ings while guiding you to charming discoveries about particular
fauna and flora, the landscape, and the local population. He sends

you along at a leisurely pace—the one he himself adopts during his sojourns on the Magdalen Islands.

Islands generally have their own peculiarities as to the diversity of species and their habitats; the Magdalens are no exception. A small territory, they have an impressive variety of natural environments. Those small parcels of land—bonsai ecosystems—are exceptionally fragile. For this reason, it is worthwhile offering advice to walkers and cyclists about how to tour the islands without damaging the often delicate envrionment.

In conservation areas, such as Pointe-de-l'Est, Île Brion, bird sanctuaries, and dune environments, conservation measures must be respected absolutely by obtaining a permit, following paths, leaving species in their natural habitats, and so on. Dunes, particularly the dune grass that holds down the sand and weaves the very framework of the dune, must not be trampled.

At no time should birds be disturbed or their surroundings disrupted. Human presence near a nest can cause adult birds to flee, and that in turn can lead to the cooling of eggs and an increase in predator activity.

The cliffs crumble very easily, so it is only prudent to stay several metres away from the edges of capes.

Apart from the public roads and paths, the dunes and beaches, most of the land is privately owned. Before crossing a fence or venturing onto private land, walkers should be sure of the owner's consent.

Another dominant feature of the island environment is, as you'll have noticed, the islanders' strong sense of belonging to their roots, their island, their archipelago. The Madelinots enjoy hearing comments about their islands from every perspective and in every accent and in comparison with other maritime regions and people. Economic and ecological concerns reflect a culture and reveal human diversity. On the Magdalens, you may hear exclamations about the temperature, questions about a lobster trap, an Acadian gable, or the scattering of houses; anger regarding the squelched seal hunt; sorrow at the malaise of the Gulf of St. Lawrence and of its families of fish.

Meeting other people is part of the pleasure and learning that walking allows, exposing us to the possibilities of a multicultural experience.

Hélène Chevrier, Ethnologist
Havre-aux-Maisons, December 1994

In 1982 I took a two-week cycling holiday that would change my life forever. From Sydney, Nova Scotia, I cycled over the majestic mountains of the Cabot Trail to the Pictou ferry on my way towards the rolling green hills of Prince Edward Island, finally arriving at the tiny port of Souris.

A dotted line on a map—indicating a ferry route—extending from Souris across the Gulf of St. Lawrence to a group of islands called the Îles-de-la-Madeleine (Magdalen Islands) was my first knowledge that this archipelago existed.

Lured by a thirst for adventure, I boarded the *Lucy Maud Montgomery* for the voyage that would take me to a place so remote it wasn't even shown on many maps of Canada!

Only five hours later, but what seemed like a million miles from civilization, I landed at the port of Cap aux Meules.

Cycling off the boat and up Chemin Débarcadère, my enthusiasm soured and turned to disillusionment as a driving rain and gusts of wind lashed at my face. Chemin Principal, the main thoroughfare, was a sea of mud with potholes, construction vehicles, flashing amber lights, and yellow barricades everywhere. I finally made it to the bed and breakfast on the outskirts of town soaked to the bone and dripping in mud. I vowed to return to P.E.I. on the first ferry the next morning!

I awoke to a gloriously sunny, warm day with not a cloud in the sky. From my window on Chemin du Marconi, I gazed in awe over the extraordinary landscape of sea, sand, and green-capped cliffs and immediately fell in love with its beauty.

In the fourteen years since then, I've returned with my family each summer to explore every corner of this captivating string of islands.

My purpose in writing this book was to share with you all the wonderful places I have discovered here over the years and to inspire you to come and find your own special places as you hike, cycle, or climb on the Magdalen Islands.

Acknowledgement

There are scores of people, who, over the past fifteen years, have shared their knowledge and love of the Îles-de-la-Madeleine (Magdalen Islands) with me and helped me discover the special places and routes described in this book.

In particular, I would like to thank Reginald Poirier, Robert Noël de Tilly, Gil Thériault, François Turbide, André Bourque, Evangeline Gaudet, Francine Leroux, Pierre Aucoin, Craig Quinn, Micheline Couture, Rémi Bergeot, Arthur Miousse, Nicole Leblanc, Hugues Massey, Yvonne Langford, Gérard Leblanc, Jean-Marc Cormier, Nicole Grégoire, and Albert Cummings. Without their assistance this book would not be possible.

Special thanks goes to Jean Boucher of Duguay and Boucher for supplying me with detailed maps of the archipelago, and to Claude Richard, who shared my enthusiasm for the book and was a constant source of encouragement and knowledge.

My sincere thanks also to Hélène Chevrier of Attention Frag'Îles and Frédéric Landry, Director of the Musée de la Mer, who graciously offered to write about the Magdalens' historical background and natural origins. Thanks, as well, to Sheila Fischman for translating their contributions into English.

Patricia Bell of Attention Frag'Îles, and Serge Bourgeois of the Municipalité Régionale du Comté des Îles-de-la-Madeleine provided valuable suggestions, corrections, and advice on the text and maps.

I thank Devora Resnick, Jean Lepage, Gertrude Morin, François LaRoche, and the hundreds of people from Sunset Bicycle Tours for their insight, patience, and advice as we climbed, cycled, and hiked each route in this book.

Last but not least, a great big thanks to my wife, Karen Green Fischer, for understanding my passion for the Magdalen Islands and persevering for over a year and a half while I spent two days every week at my computer.

The Magdalen Islands' History

The Mi'kmaq

There is evidence to suggest that Mi'kmaq were present in the Magdalen Islands about four thousand years ago. An abundance of relics and concentrations of artifacts and stone debris testify to their passage here. Skilled navigators, they plied the coasts of the Gulf of St. Lawrence in search of fish and sea mammals. When Europeans arrived, there were more signs of Mi'kmaq population along the coastline. In 1597, on his ship the *Hopewell*, Charles Leigh hunted walrus near the Magdalen Islands. Upon entering a harbour with the Mi'kmaq name "Halabolina," he was attacked by French sailors and some three hundred Amerindians.

The Discoverers

Canada had already been officially discovered by Jacques Cartier, who reached the Magdalen Islands on June 24, 1534, by the time Samuel de Champlain passed close to the Rocher aux Oiseaux in 1608. He had trouble identifying the three islets Cartier had mentioned in his accounts of his voyages. Champlain drew a map on which the name Îles aux Gros Yeux identified the archipelago known today as the Magdalen Islands.

The Colonizers

The first seigneur of the islands was Nicolas Denys, who received his title in 1653. He also had establishments in Nova Scotia. Every year his ships came to the islands to fish and to hunt seals and walrus.

In 1663 the Compagnie de la Nouvelle-France conceded the title of Seigneur des Îles Ramées to François Doublet, a ship's captain from Honfleur. That same year he armed two ships, the *Saint-Michel* and the *Grenadier*. In addition to the crews, he had with him twenty-five men who were to settle the islands. To mark taking possession of his seigneury, when he arrived at the islands he planted a cross on the highest cape, at the entrance to the port at Havre-Aubert.

Doublet went back to France then returned to visit his colony towards the end of June in 1664. He was shocked to find that all his property had been destroyed and his men had deserted and gone on to Quebec. This marked the end of a commendable attempt at settlement. All that remained of his rule was the islands' French name, Îles-de-la-Madeleine,

bestowed on them by Doublet in honour of his wife, Madeleine Fontaine.

The Magdalen Islands were subsequently granted to various companies or individuals, who took advantage of their fishing or hunting rights during the summer but had little or no interest in advancing the settlement.

Grand Pré

After the Acadians at Grand Pré were deported to the Anglo-American colonies in 1755, there was concern among Acadians elsewhere. Many of them took flight and scattered along the coasts of New Brunswick, Gaspé, and Île Saint-Jean (now Prince Edward Island). Some had already arrived at Cape Breton Island.

Gathering the Acadians

In 1761 Acadians from Île Saint-Jean and possibly some from the Baie des Chaleurs found sanctuary in the Magdalen Islands. Others came in 1765 and settled at Havre-Aubert. Most of them worked for Richard Gridley, an Anglo-American who had settled on the islands once peace was established and set up a station for hunting walrus and seals. He had brought other Acadians with him. Twenty-two of Gridley's enlisted men—seventeen Acadians and five French Canadians—took the oath of allegiance to Britain on August 31, 1763.

After the British conquest of Quebec in 1759, the Magdalen Islands were annexed to Newfoundland for administrative purposes. With the Quebec Act of 1774, the islands passed to the jurisdiction of Lower Canada and were united with Quebec.

Miquelonnais on the Magdalen Islands

In 1792 Miquelon's population departed to Cape Breton and the Magdalen Islands during a time of intense rivalry between the European French and English over the abundant supply of fish around Saint-Pierre and Miquelon. Two hundred and twenty-three individuals, under their spiritual leader Abbé Jean-Baptiste Allain, arrived at Havre-Aubert in the spring of 1792. They came to join their fellow Miquelonnais who had been scattered to the four corners of the country following struggles for conquest between France and England. They were welcomed warmly by other Acadians who had arrived before them.

It was then that the Acadians of the Magdalen Islands formed

a civil and religious community. In small groups they scattered across the islands to the coves and shorelines that would prove profitable for fishing a variety of species. The territory was divided so that each settler could cultivate a plot of land. Although life was harsh and strenuous, they became attached to these surroundings, where they had finally found an oasis of peace.

Today the Acadians of the Magdalen Islands, in association with English-speaking fishermen from the neighbouring Maritime provinces and elsewhere, form a vibrant, hospitable community for the many foreign visitors who flock here during the tourist season every year. Tourists come for the excellent climate, for the white sand beaches linking the islands, and for the abundant marine flora and fauna. It is a remote paradise both for year-round inhabitants and for all the visitors who travel here.

Frédéric Landry
Director, Musée de la Mer

Îles-de-la-Madeleine

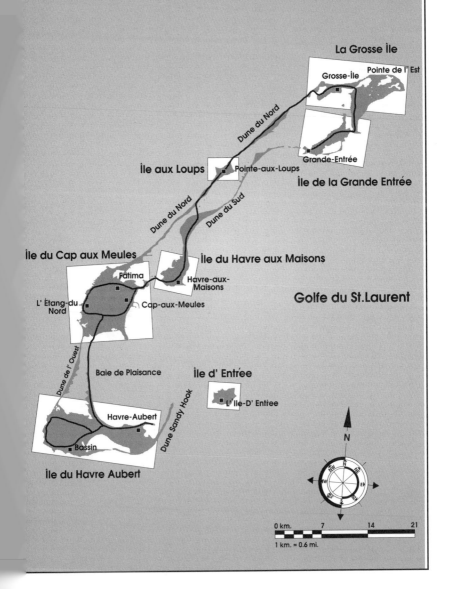

La Grosse Île

Pointe de l' Est

Grosse-Île

Grande-Entrée

Île de la Grande Entrée

Dune du Nord

Île aux Loups

Pointe-aux-Loups

Dune du Nord

Dune du Sud

Île du Cap aux Meules

Île du Havre aux Maisons

Fatima

Havre-aux-Maisons

L' Étang-du-Nord

Cap-aux-Meules

Golfe du St.Laurent

Dune de l' Ouest

Baie de Plaisance

Île d' Entrée

L' Île-D' Entrée

Havre-Aubert

Dune Sandy Hook

Bassin

Île du Havre Aubert

N

0 km.   7   14   21

1 km. = 0.6 mi.

Travelling to the Magdalen Islands
(Îles-de-la-Madeleine)

The very first thing you should do when planning your visit to the Magdalen Islands is contact either Tourisme Québec or the Association Touristique des Îles-de-la-Madeleine (the Tourist Bureau) to obtain the tourist guide.

This wonderful guide has everything you'll need to know about accommodations, restaurants, camp sites, museums, car rentals, guided tours, scenic cruises, and much more—including detailed road maps for each of the populated islands.

To obtain the guide, contact: Association Touristique des Îles-de-la-Madeleine, C.P. 1028 Cap-aux-Meules, Îles-de-la-Madeleine, Quebec, GOB 1BO, Canada. Tel: (418) 986-2245. Fax: (418) 986-2327.

Association Touristique des Îles—the Tourist Bureau—is at the corner of Chemin Principal (Route 199) and Chemin du Débarcadère—just up the road from the ferry terminal. The office is open every day from June 24 until Labour Day, (7:00 a.m. to 9:00 p.m.). The staff are a great help in finding accommodations—whether you're looking for a hotel, bed and breakfast, or camp site. Try to avoid the office when the ferry comes in (between 7:00 and 8:00 p.m. daily). It's an absolute madhouse with hordes of people descending on the tiny building.

From March on, the office also takes telephone reservations for accommodations. Just phone, tell them your arrival and departure date, and they'll handle the rest—no charge.

You can also get information about the Magdalen Islands—including the guide book—by contacting Tourisme Québec, Case Postale 20,000, Québec City, Quebec, Canada, G1K 7X2. Toll Free 1-800-363-7777 (Monday through Friday 9:00 a.m. to 5:00 p.m.).

There are a number of ways to reach the islands depending on your budget and schedule.

By Car and Passenger Ferry
From Souris, Prince Edward Island

Taking the ferry—the *Lucy Maud Montgomery*—is by far the most popular way to get to the islands. A sea voyage is a great way to unwind and gradually adjust your city-paced mentality to the more relaxed island way of life. You sail up the eastern coast of Prince Edward Island, past the East Point Lighthouse and then out into the Gulf of St. Lawrence, where you might even catch a glimpse of some whales. There's a lounge, cafeteria, gift

shop, and children's centre on board, and the first mate will be glad to give you a tour of the bridge or the engine room.

In season (from mid-June to mid-September) the ferry leaves Souris at 2:00 p.m. every day (except Tuesday) and arrives in Cap-aux-Meules approximately five hours later. Departure time from Cap-aux-Meules is at 8:00 a.m. each day, except Tuesday when it is 8:00 p.m. There are extra crossings from July 1 to August 15, when the ferry leaves Souris at 2:00 a.m. and leaves from Cap-aux-Meules at 8:00 p.m.

The ferry can transport approximately ninety vehicles and four hundred passengers. During the summer it's often filled, so it's a good idea to make reservations early—especially if you plan to visit in July or August.

For reservations contact C.T.M.A. (Coopérative de Transport Maritime et Aérien), Cap-aux-Meules (418) 986-3278. They'll need the make of your car, license number, and arrival and departure dates as well as a deposit made by credit card.

For further information or prices phone Cap-aux-Meules, (418) 986-6600, or Souris, (P.E.I.), (902) 687-2181.

By Cargo ship from Montréal

(You can take your car as well)

This is one of the most adventurous ways of getting to the islands. Sailing up the St. Lawrence River aboard the C.T.M.A. *Voyageur* for two days is a unique experience.

The *Voyageur* leaves Montréal every Friday (in season) at about 5:00 p.m. and docks Sunday afternoon in the Magdalens. Since the ship carries only fifteen passengers you have to book at least two months in advance. The return voyage leaves on Wednesday and arrives in Montréal on Friday.

For information about prices and reservations phone Cap-aux-Meules (418) 986-6600, or Montréal (514) 937-7656.

By Passenger Ferry from Chéticamp, Nova Scotia

The *Macassa Bay* sails daily from Chéticamp, Nova Scotia (Cape Breton), at 7:30 a.m. and docks at Havre-Aubert about five hours later (from July 1 to September 5). The boat carries approximately one hundred passengers—who can bring their windsurfers and bicycles—but no cars. The *Macassa Bay* departs from Havre-Aubert at 2:30 p.m. and arrives back in Chéticamp around 7:00 p.m.

For further information contact Marine Acadie Limitée, Chéticamp, Nova Scotia. Toll free 1-800-866-2343.

By Plane

If you're short on time, there are several flight options. If you're calling a travel agent outside of Quebec the hardest part of the reservation process will be for the agent to find the correct airline coding for the Magdalen Islands. It's YGR. That should save you some time!

Air Alliance

An Air Alliance thirty-eight-seat Dash 8 flies out of Montréal, with another Air Alliance connection in Québec City. From Québec City you can take a direct flight and arrive in the Magdalens about two hours later, or take the scenic route—stopping in Mont-Joli and Gaspé and arrive in the islands four hours later.

For further information and reservations call Quebec (Toll Free) 1-800-361-8620; Îles-de-la-Madeline (418) 969-2888; or Montréal (514) 393-3333.

Inter-Canadian

Inter-Canadian flies the same route as Air Alliance aboard a forty-four-seat A.T.R. plane.

For further information and reservations call Quebec (Toll Free) 1-800-361-0200; Îles-de-la-Madeleine (418) 969-2764; or Montréal (514) 847-2211.

Using this Guidebook

Each chapter in this book is devoted to a different island—starting with Grande Entrée in the north, and ending with Île d'Entrée to the south. At the beginning of each chapter there is an overview map showing the general location of each cycling, hiking, and climbing route and the number assigned to that particular route. For each route marked on the overview map there is a detailed map—to scale—indicating the scenic sites and landmarks along the way.

Each detailed map is followed by important basic facts about the hiking route (route distance, approximate time required, terrain, road conditions, difficulty, suitability, precautions, what to wear/bring, when to go, facilities, points of interest, directions to route starting point) and a narrative description that explains how to follow the route. I've also provided some background information on the surrounding landscape, geography, history, shipwrecks, and anything else I consider interesting or unique about the route.

At the end of every chapter is a map pointing to Other Adventures to be found on the island, followed by a description of each activity.

There are eleven hiking routes, ten climbing routes, and six cycling routes in all. They range from a challenging 7.4 km (4.6 mi.) hike around the perimeter of Île d'Entrée to a leisurely .4 km (.25 mi.) climb to the summit of Butte chez Mounette. The sixteen Other Adventures range from horseback riding to scuba diving.

Directions to the starting point of every route (including the Other Adventures) begin at the Tourist Bureau—located at the intersection of Highway 199 and Chemin du Débarcadère in Cap-aux-Meules, near where the *Lucy Maud Montgomery* docks.

All the maps in this guidebook were drawn up by me after hiking, cycling, or climbing each route. Although I've made every effort to be precise about distance measurements, landmarks, and sites, I apologize in advance for any changes that have occurred since I wrote this book. Over the years a cliff formation will collapse, a shipwreck will disappear, a grocery store will close. Please let me know of any changes you discover and I'll incorporate them into revised editions.

Climbing Route		Birdwatching area	
Cycling Route		Birdwatching area	
Hiking Route		Birdwatching area	
Church		Seals	
Grocery/Restaurant		Cows	
Mine\Hydro Plant		Clamdigging	
Lighthouse		Cross on Mountain	
Hay Baraque		Summit	
Camping Area		Bridge	
Small House		Picnic Area	
Hospital		Conservation Area	
Tourist Bureau		Snorkelling/Scuba Diving	
Parking Area		Wagon	
Large Building		Cemetery	
Local Airport		Platform	
Main Airport		Forest	
Helipad		Gas Station	
Small Boat		Descriptive Panel	
Ferry Terminal		Fencing	
Shipwreck		Rope and Stake	
Fishing Boat		Boardwalk	
Harbour/Port		Playground	
Direction Sign		Dolos	
Direction Sign		Car Wreck	
Direction Sign		Highway Number	
Danger Sign		Scenic Site	
		Adventure Operator	
		Telephone Pole	

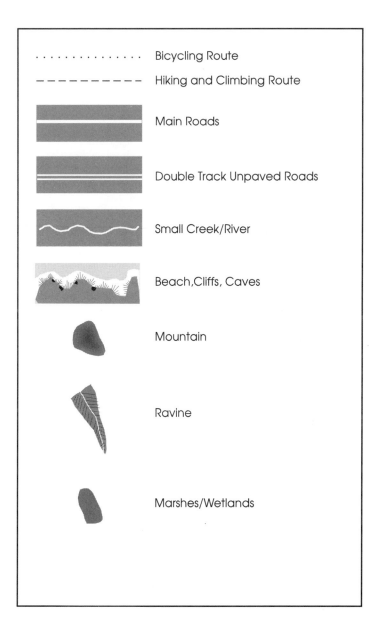

· · · · · · · · · · · · · · Bicycling Route

– – – – – – – – – – Hiking and Climbing Route

Main Roads

Double Track Unpaved Roads

Small Creek/River

Beach,Cliffs, Caves

Mountain

Ravine

Marshes/Wetlands

Special Tips

Listed below are some points to remember when undertaking the routes described in this book.

Private Land

Several of the routes partially traverse on private land—Hiking Route 2: Île Boudreau to Chemin des Pealey in Chapter 2; Climbing Route 3: Cap du Dauphin in Chapter 3; Climbing Route 5: Les Buttes Pelées in Chapter 5; and Hiking Route 2: La Belle Anse to Cap au Trou in Chapter 6. Most islanders are happy to share the beauty of their island with you and will not mind if you hike on their land, so long as you stay on the trail and respect their property. However, if you meet the property owner while you're hiking, please ask whether you can finish your hike and then respect their wishes.

Hiking

On the hiking routes try to stay on marked paths and established trails so as to avoid trampling on rare or endangered vegetation.

Cliffs

Many of the hikes are along cliffs that are extremely unstable and can crumble beneath you. You should stay at least 9 m (30 ft.) from the cliff ledges for safety's sake.

Wildflowers and Plants

Feel free to pick field strawberries, but please don't collect plants or wildflowers. Leave all vegetation in its natural habitat.

Swimming

Many of the beaches in the Magdalen Islands have dangerous underwater currents and undertows—particularly the Plage de la Grande Échouerie, Dune du Nord, Île Boudreau, Dune du Sud, and Plage de l'Ouest. The current can quickly pull you away from shore, therefore it's best not to swim alone and to stay close to shore.

Water

Don't drink water from ponds or streams.

Weather

The weather here can change suddenly, and you should be prepared for warm sunshine and rain all in the same day. What you see in the morning may not forecast the whole day!

Refuse

Don't leave any garbage behind anywhere. I often carry a backpack with a plastic bag in it for my garbage, until I find a garbage receptacle.

Forests

The forests on the Magdalens are extremely fragile. Please don't make any fires while hiking, as an accident could destroy the forests.

Mosquitoes

Mosquito numbers are unpredictable here, but it's wise to carry repellent—especially for many of the climbing routes—just in case.

Bird Nesting Grounds

Avoid the nesting grounds of birds. The Piping Plover—an endangered species—nests on beaches, and in some places there are signs and fences indicating their nesting grounds. Please don't enter these restricted areas.

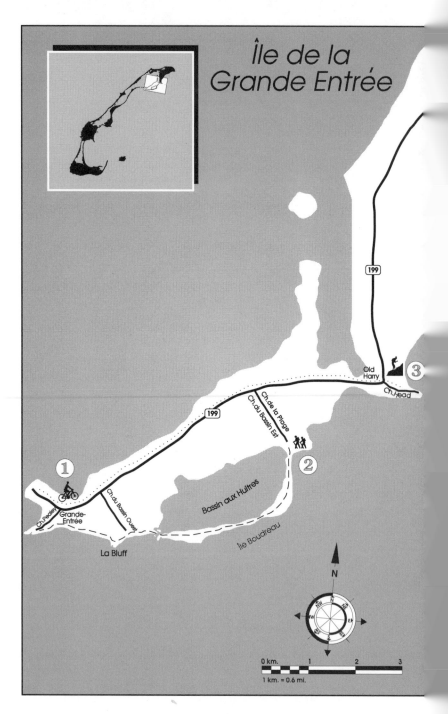

Île de la Grande Entrée

199

Old Harry

Ch. Head

③

Ch. de la Plage

Ch. du Bassin Est

199

①

Ch. Pedley

Grande-Entrée

Ch. du Bassin Ouest

②

Bassin aux Huîtres

Île Boudreau

La Bluff

N

0 km.   1   2   3

1 km. ≈ 0.6 mi.

Grande-Entrée to Pointe Old-Harry

Route Length:
11.4 km (7 mi.) one way and 20.5 km (12.7 mi.) if you decide to
return to Grande-Entrée. (No detours on the way back.)

Approximate Time Required:
It's about a forty-five-minute ride, but exploring the sites along
the route, can easily stretch it to two hours. Add another forty-
five minutes if you're riding back to Grande-Entrée.

Terrain:
The cycling is about as flat as it can get, with one or two small
hills that shouldn't even require a gear change—if you're in
reasonable shape.

Road Conditions:
The road's paved the whole way, and traffic is light. In the
summer the winds generally blow from the southwest at 17-40
km/h (10-25 mph) and help speed your progress towards Old-
Harry. But don't count on the winds.

Difficulty:
Anyone who does a bit of exercise should have no trouble
completing the ride.

Facilities:
There are refreshments and washrooms along the way, and
they're shown on the map.

Points of Interest:
Don't miss these sights, which are shown on the map Cycling
Route 1: 1) shipwreck of the *Nadine* in Grande-Entrée Harbour,
craft shops of Grande-Entrée and lobster factory; 2) cliffs, caves,
and grottoes at the end of Chemin des Pealey; 3) Seal
Interpretation Centre at Club vacances "Les Îles"; 4) Baie Old-
Harry, where seacows were slaughtered in the 1800s; 5) one-
room Old-Harry Schoolhouse, built in 1921; 6) harbour at Old-
Harry; 7) the Plage de la Grande Échouerie (beach).

Directions to Route Starting Point:

From the tourist office, turn right on Chemin Principal following signs for 199 East towards Havre-aux-Maisons, Pointe-aux-Loups, Grosse-Île, and Grande-Entrée. Stay on 199 East until the road ends at the harbour of Grande-Entrée. Straight ahead you' ll see a blue and grey fishing trawler—the *Nadine*. From the Tourist Bureau to here's about 59 km (35 mi.)—forty minutes by car. The cycling route begins here.

Route Description:

0.0 km (0.0 mi.)   The Pointe de la Grande Entrée, where the *Nadine* rests, is the last inch of Highway 199.

On the night of December 16, 1990, the *Nadine* sank in a storm about ten miles off the coast of Grande-Entrée. There were two survivors, three missing, and eight dead in this maritime tragedy—one of the worst in recent history. There was a federal inquiry into the mishap; the ship was raised and towed to Grande-Entrée Harbour, where investigators searched for clues to the sinking.

The tiny sand island just across the channel is home to many bird species including the endangered Piping Plover and Arctic Terns. The Arctic Tern is easily recognizable by its blood-red bill and black cap. The Piping Plover blends in with the sandy beach and is harder to see without binoculars.

Traditional Acadian architecture near Grand Entrée.

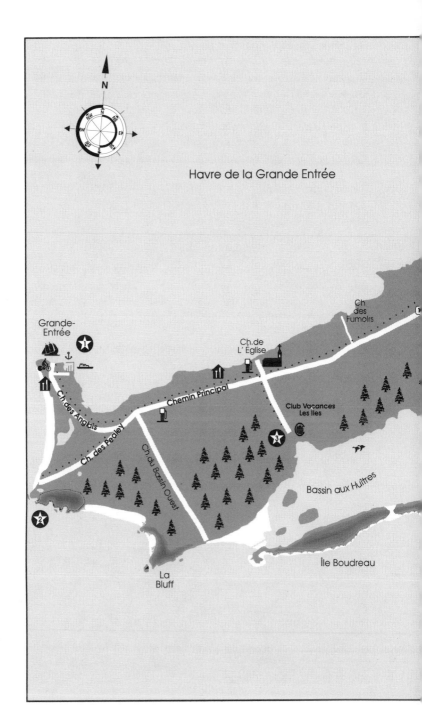

Havre de la Grande Entrée

Grande-
Entrée

Ch. des Anglais

Ch. des Pealey

Chemin Principal

Ch. de
L' Eglise

Ch
des
Fumoirs

Club Vacances
Les Iles

Ch. du Bassin Ouest

Bassin aux Huîtres

Île Boudreau

La
Bluff

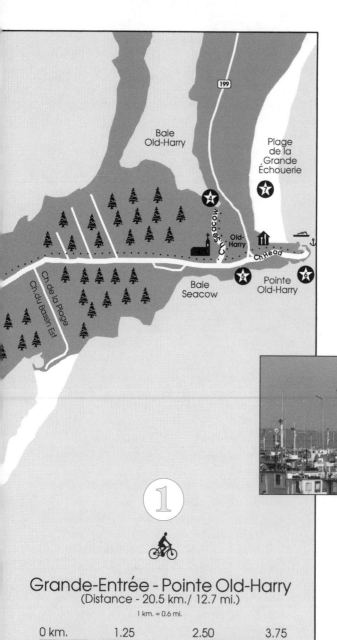

Baie
Old-Harry

Plage
de la
Grande
Échouerie

Old-
Harry

Baie
Seacow

Pointe
Old-Harry

Ch. Seacow

Ch. Head

Ch. de la plage

Ch. du Bassin Est

199

①

Grande-Entrée - Pointe Old-Harry
(Distance - 20.5 km./ 12.7 mi.)

1 km. = 0.6 mi.

| 0 km. | 1.25 | 2.50 | 3.75 |

*Colourful harbour of
Grande-Entrée crammed with
brightly painted fishing boats.*

In Grande-Entrée, visit the local craft shop, Souvenirs Pol des Îles, which sells island souvenirs, and the boutique Au Tour de la Terre for it's handmade pottery. Grande Entrée, the last island in the archipelago to be settled (in the late 1800s) has been called the Lobster Capital of the World. Its tiny harbour is crammed with fishing boats. If it's lobster season (May 10 to July 10), a visit to the Madelimer Inc. fish processing plant (opposite the *Nadine*) to see the lobster holding tanks is worth the trip. An annual Lobster Festival is held here in late July. There's outdoor entertainment and, of course, lobster suppers.

1.1 km (.7 mi.)   Cycle along 199 West to a fork in the road. Turn right onto Chemin des Pealey and follow the road till the end. You'll see a parking area and picnic bench on the right.

Leave your bicycle here and walk to the beach. Looking east, you'll see a trail winding along the cliff tops. Walking along the trail, you'll see the devastating effects of erosion. Relentless wave action has carved magnificent grottoes and caves into the red sandstone cliffs. The headlands, cliffs, and vegetation in the area are extremely fragile, so stay on the path that is bordered by rope and stakes.

2.8 km (1.7 mi.)   Follow Chemin des Pealey back to Highway 199. At the Stop sign turn right onto 199 West.

5.2 km (3.1 mi.)   Continue on 199 West. Just past the Action Plus grocery store turn right onto a dirt road that leads to Club vacances "Les Îles."

At the Club vacances "Les Îles" (an adventure/nature complex and hotel for hikers and outdoor enthusiasts) you can visit the Seal Interpretation Centre, probably the best place in Quebec to learn about seals. It features interactive displays depicting their history, habitat, and life cycles. Its large library contains books, audio visual material, and scientific studies of seals. Kids and adults alike are fascinated by the interactive displays. The centre is in the hotel just around the corner from the cafeteria. It's open weekdays from 9:00 a.m. to 7:00 p.m. and weekends from 10:00 a.m. to 5:00 p.m.

A self-interpretive panel behind the hotel describes the type of forest that can be found on Grande Entrée and the importance of trees to the island's ecosystem for soil conservation and ground

water. Alder thickets, which are abundant on Grande Entrée, play a crucial role in soil stabilization and create conditions that promote the growth of fir and spruce seeds.

The islands were once heavily forested, but the demand for houses, boats, and firewood—coupled with poor soil and strong winds—have reduced forest coverage to stunted spruce and fir that cover only about 18 per cent of the archipelago.

8.4 km (5.2 mi.)   From the Club vacances "Les Îles" return to Highway 199 and turn right onto 199 West. After about 3 km (1.8 mi.) you'll see on your left the St. Peter's by the Sea Church.

This church—the oldest Anglican church on the Magdalen Islands—has beautiful stained glass windows. The carved wooden entrance doors are a memorial to Aaron Clark, who drowned while saving two swimmers dragged out by the undertow at Plage de la Grande Échouerie. He was awarded the Order of Canada posthumously. There is also a wooden sculpture, erected in July 1984, honouring the arrival here of Jacques Cartier in 1534. The tombstones in the graveyard show the long line of Clarks and Dunns who settled this area.

Church on Grande Entrée.

9.5 km (5.8 mi.)   Turn left off 199 onto Chemin Seacow Path and follow the road till it stops at Baie Old-Harry (Old-Harry Bay).

According to local historian and archaeologist Leonard Clark, Old-Harry Bay was where walruses were slaughtered. Their poor vision made them easy prey for hunters. In 1765 over two

thousand were shot on the beaches of the bay. Walking along the shoreline, you may find some bones of these large animals or the musket balls used to shoot them in the back of the head.

In Old-Harry Bay, and other such harbours, the hunters would cut up the walruses for their skins, blubber, and ivory and load them onto ships anchored nearby.

There's a 2-km (1.2-mi.) walk along the east side of the bay that takes you opposite the island of Îles aux Loups Marins—a bird-lover's paradise, filled with Double-crested Cormorants, Great Black-backed Gulls, Herring Gulls, and Great Blue Herons.

10.1 km (6.1 mi.) Return to the Stop sign at the intersection of Chemin Seacow Path and 199 West, turn left onto Highway 199.

10.2 km (6.2 mi.) Stop on your right at the little red house—Old-Harry Schoolhouse.

The Old-Harry School is a fascinating place to visit. This one-room schoolhouse was built in 1921 and was operational until 1973. The Council for Anglophone Magdalen Islanders (CAMI) made it a museum depicting anglophone heritage and culture. Interesting artifacts, old photographs, books, and letters evoke lives and times gone by.

10.5 km (6.4 mi.) Stay on Highway 199 until the fork in the road. Turn right onto Chemin Head. (The sign's a little faded and hard to read.)

11.4 km (7 mi.) Arrive at the harbour of Old-Harry.

The port at Old-Harry—named after Old Harry Head near Portsmouth, England—is one of the most picturesque on the islands. The large pile of concrete blocks beside the pier are called dolosse, a South African word meaning the knuckle bone of a sheep. I presume that's what their unusual shape resembles. They're used as a breakwater to protect the harbour and prevent erosion. From the cliffs at Pointe Old-Harry, the white sands of Plage de la Grande Échouerie stretch as far as the eye can see. It's considered by many to be the most beautiful beach on the Magdalens.

From Pointe Old-Harry, Newfoundland is only 243 km (150 mi.) to the east. In the 1700s these beaches, or échoueries, were home to tens of thousands of walruses. (Imagine them rolling and

jostling for space on the beaches.) The slaughter by Europeans and Americans in the eighteenth century wiped out the walrus in these islands.

Don't miss the caves and grottoes chiselled out by the sea near the point and the precarious perches of nesting guillemots and cormorants.

If it's a warm, sunny day, take a walk and a swim on Plage de la Grande Échouerie. (The Pointe-de-l'Est National Wildlife Reserve borders the beach.) It's an ideal place for a picnic and a great spot for kite flying. To get onto the beach, follow Chemin Head back to the intersection of Highway 199. Just past the little snack bar turn right onto Old-Harry Beach Road.

The water at Grande Échouerie can be very fresh—17°C (63°F) is about average. Watch out for the dangerous undercurrents that can pull you out to sea. Near the cliffs is a memorial plaque to Aaron Clark who drowned here while saving two swimmers caught in the undertow.

There's a more detailed description and climbing route of Old-Harry on page 29 (Pointe Old-Harry Climbing Route 3).

20.5 km (12.7 mi.) Return along 199 East to Grande-Entrée

Île Boudreau to Chemin des Pealey

Route Length:
Once you reach Chemin des Pealey you'll have hiked 5.6 km (3.5 mi.). If you're feeling energetic you can return along the same trail, a distance of 11.2 km (7 mi.). My preference is often to walk to the intersection of Chemin des Pealey and 199 and hitchhike back to Chemin du Bassin East. Usually, I don't have to wait more than five minutes to get a ride from one of the friendly Madelinots. Most islanders go out of their way to drop me off at my car. But be prepared to walk back!

Approximate Time Required:
It should take about two hours to reach Chemin des Pealey and another two more for the return trip. If you get a ride back along Highway 199, it'll take you five to ten minutes.

Terrain:
About half the hike's along the beach and the rest on clifftops overlooking the sea. On the beaches you might find it easier to walk barefoot and as near to the sea as possible. The sand's firmer closer to the water, so you won't sink in as deep. The highest point along the route is about 24 m (80 ft.). On the plateaus and cliffs there's a visible path.

Bluffs near Chemin des Pealey.

Difficulty:

This walk can be taken by just about anyone, but there are two places that require climbing (both up and down) a 9-m (30-ft.) slope that's not very steep. There's a rope in both spots to help you. When you're going down, stay as vertical as you can and look over your shoulder to see the path behind you.

Precautions:

Stay away from the edge of the cliffs. They're very unstable. Climb slowly when using the ropes and make sure your footing is secure. Be careful not to disturb any Piping Plovers that are seen nesting on the beaches, and don't pick any endangered plants.

What to Wear/Bring:

A pair of shorts or a bathing suit (for those quick dips in the sea) and a sturdy pair of walking shoes. Binoculars will help if you're watching for seals or Piping Plovers.

When to Go:

I like early morning. The sun accentuates the redness of the cliffs and there's to be an abundance of bird life in Bassin aux Huîtres. But any time of day is good, provided you leave enough time to get back before dark.

Points of Interest:

The island of Île Boudreau; the cliffs and rock formations at Chemin des Pealey; opportunities to see the endangered Piping Plover in it's natural habitat.

Directions to Route Starting Point:

From the Tourist Bureau, turn right on Chemin Principal. Follow signs for 199 East, which takes you to Havre-aux-Maisons, Pointe-aux-Loups, Grosse-Île, and then Grande-Entrée. Shortly after passing Old-Harry you'll turn left onto a dirt road—Chemin du Bassin Est (also called Chemin de la Plage). Follow it to the end, take the fork to the right and park there. Don't go too far along the fork as you may get stuck, and the area is ecologically fragile. It's about 58 km (36 mi.)—forty-five minutes by car.

Route Description:

Each Monday, come rain or shine, Micheline, Ulysses (our dog), and I

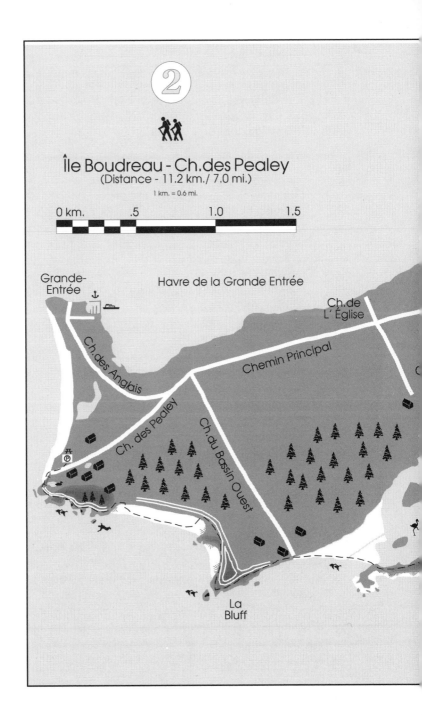

② 🚶🚶

Île Boudreau - Ch.des Pealey
(Distance - 11.2 km./ 7.0 mi.)

1 km. = 0.6 mi.

0 km.   .5   1.0   1.5

Grande-
Entrée

Havre de la Grande Entrée

Ch.de
L' Église

Ch.des Anglais

Chemin Principal

Ch. des Pealey

Ch.du Bassin Ouest

La
Bluff

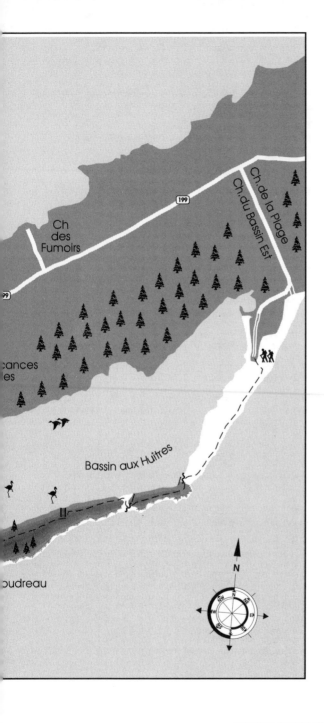

drive straight for Île Boudreau. Along our way we don't stop at the magnificent beaches of Pointe-aux-Loups or Grosse-Île. Not a longing glance is cast at the famous Grande Échouerie beach or Old-Harry. We're headed straight to the little parking space at the end of Chemin du Bassin Est, our favourite spot for doing what we enjoy the most— absolutely nothing!

Of course, absolutely nothing, for us, means lazily strolling along a cliff-top path bursting with a myriad of flowers, from yellow silver-weed to purple irises. As we walk, we gaze alternatively at the calm bay of Bassin aux Huîtres on one side and the wild open sea on the other. On each visit to our special place we discover a new land-scape—a field filled with the aroma of wild strawberries, which we spend the afternoon sampling, or a meadow, white with daisies, where we enjoy a picnic lunch and watch Ulysses chasing the gulls.

It was these observations by Galerie d'Art Point-Sud owners, Micheline Couture and Rémi Bergeot, that inspired me to visit Île Boudreau and develop the following route.

Just twenty years ago, Île Boudreau was still a monolithic cape that stretched into the sea, creating the partially closed body of water—Bassin aux Huîtres. Fierce winter winds and erosion have since sliced the cape into two sections.

From Bassin aux Huîtres walk east towards the sound of the crashing waves. When you reach the beach and face southwards you'll see the green-capped plateaus of Île Boudreau. Continue walking south.

More than 30 per cent of the Magdalen Islands are covered by sand. If you find walking difficult, try closer to the water's edge where the sand's more firmly packed. But take your shoes off— for obvious reasons.

As you walk towards Île Boudreau, you may see a few grey seals curiously watching you from the sea. This beach is consid-ered to be a nesting area for the endangered Piping Plover. The environmental group Attention Frag'Îles suggests that if you see one you make a wide detour to avoid trampling its eggs. Please obey any posted signs and cordoned off areas.

The Piping Plover was placed on the endangered species list in 1985. In 1987 there were just over thirty-five pairs left in Quebec, and the Magdalen Islands were the only known breeding location in Quebec. Plovers eat mainly insects and small crustaceans, and nest on beaches. They usually lay four eggs in a small depression

in the ground between May 1 and August 15. Both the plover and its eggs blend in well with the sand and stones, so it's easy to trample the eggs by accident. Using binoculars can help you spot these small, sand-coloured birds.

When you reach Île Boudreau, you'll find a rope on the Bassin aux Huîtres side to help you climb to the plateau above. The ascent is about 15 m (50 ft.), but it's not very steep and is quite manageable. The red sandstone is very unstable and crumbly.

Île Boudreau is composed of red sandstone, clay, and volcanic rock. The pink and white veins running through the sandstone are gypsum. The sandstone is red due to the iron oxide in it. When eroded by the wind and waves, it leaves behind quartz—or all the sand and dunes you're seeing.

Ascending the slopes of Île Boudreau.

When you reach the end of the first section of Île Boudreau you'll find a rope to help you descend from the plateau to the beach. (The rope is on the side facing the sea.) Be very cautious on your way down, and get secure footholds.

When you have reached the beach, cross over to the Bassin aux Huîtres side and climb up to the second section of Île Boudreau. The climb's pretty easy, but there's no rope to help you this time.

When you get to the top of the second cape follow the marked path through fields of silverweed and irises. At the end of July the plateau is bursting with field strawberries.

The Bassin aux Huîtres, on your right, is often filled with Blue Herons fishing for supper—particularly at low tide. When you

reach the stairs and dock for the Club vacances "Les Îles," you're halfway across Île Boudreau.

At the end of Île Boudreau, you'll see a large colony of Black-backed Gulls. Follow the beach across the narrow portion of Bassin aux Huîtres. There may be a shallow tidal river that you'll have to wade across if it's high tide. This stretch of beach is a Piping Plover nesting ground, so walk along the water's edge between May and August to avoid disturbing them. Two endangered plants, the Gulf of St. Lawrence Aster *(Aster Laurentianus)* and Spurred Gentian *(Halenia Deflexa)* grow in the small open fields just behind the beaches, but I hope you won't pick any plants.

Near the end of the beach you'll pass a house at the foot of Chemin du Bassin Ouest. Continue past it along the path to La Bluff, where there are some spectacular small islands and rock formations. It's also a nesting ground for Black Guillemots and Double-crested Cormorants, which feed on the small fish and crustaceans found on the coastline.

You'll have no difficulty identifying the Black Guillemot—distinctive bright red feet, black plumage, and large white patches on their wings. The Double-crested Cormorant's long neck and slender body make it look a bit like a crow. The word cormorant comes from the latin *Corvus Marinus,* or sea crow.

Just past La Bluff, the route descends along a sandy path to the beach, then climbs back up alongside an alder thicket.

This last stretch of beach is a good spot to collect souvenirs from the sea. Curious pieces of driftwood, razorshells, starfish, sand dollars, moon shells, or cockles make wonderful mementos.

The caves and rock formations at the end of this beach are a popular destination for skin divers from the Club vacances "Les Îles."

Climb up the path at the end of the beach to the cliffs of Chemin des Pealey. The rest of the route is along a path bordered by a rope and posts to protect the cliffs and vegetation from erosion. This remaining portion of the route is along private land, so don't wander off the path.

The path winds along the cliff tops past a small pond—often filled with ducks and grebes. You'll cross an opening in the fence, and then it's a short walk along the beach to Chemin des Pealey.

From here you can retrace your steps, or hitchhike back from the intersection of Highway 199 and Chemin des Pealey.

Pointe Old-Harry

Route Length:
This short, circular route is about .8 km (.5 mi.).

Approximate Time Required:
To hike this route takes about thirty minutes, but if you stop at the Plage de la Grande Échouerie you may spend the whole day at Old-Harry swimming on this magnificent beach.

Terrain:
On most of this hike you'll be walking along the cliffs of Pointe Old-Harry and Seacow Bay. This route doesn't have a well-defined trail, but sometimes you'll see a path—particularly at Pointe Old-Harry and along Seacow Bay.

Difficulty:
Anyone can do it, but watch children along the cliffs.

Precautions:
Some of the cliffs are 15 m (50 ft.) high, and they're unstable. To be on the safe side, stay at least 5 m (15 ft.) from the edges.

What to Wear/Bring:
Parts of the route go through tall grass that can scratch your legs, so I suggest long pants. Shorts are fine if you feel tough. Bring a bathing suit, in case you want to swim at the Old-Harry beach. If you're a birdwatcher, bring binoculars. There are great opportunities to see nesting Double-crested Cormorants and Black Guillemots on the cliffs.

When to Go:
Any time of the day.

Points of Interest:
Tiny picturesque fishing harbour of Old-Harry; cliffs, grottoes, and caves around Pointe Old-Harry; magnificent views of the Plage de la Grande Échouerie and most easterly point of the islands—Pointe de l'Est; large dolosse used to prevent cliff erosion and used as a breakwater.

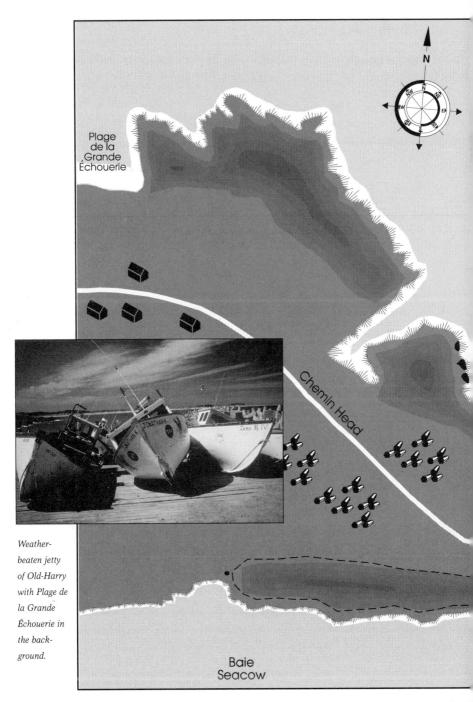

Plage
de la
Grande
Échouerie

N

Chemin Head

Weather-
beaten jetty
of Old-Harry
with Plage de
la Grande
Échouerie in
the back-
ground.

Baie
Seacow

Pointe Old - Harry
(Distance - .8 km./.5 mi.)

1 km. = 0.6 mi.

| 0 km. | .05 | .10 | .15 |

Directions to Route Starting Point:

From the Tourist Bureau, turn right on Chemin Principal following signs for 199 East, through Havre-aux-Maisons, Pointe-aux-Loups, and Grosse-Île. Several kilometres past the large blue sign for Pointe-de-l'Est National Wildlife Reserve, Highway 199 veers sharply right, towards Grande-Entrée. At this intersection, turn left onto Chemin Head. (The sign is faded and hard to read.) Continue to the harbour. It's about 53 km (32 mi.)—a half-hour by car.

Route Description:

If you ask the locals how Old-Harry got its name, most will tell you that "An old man named Harry" lived in the area. Some say it was named after Harry Clark—for a long time the only resident. According to Magdalen Island historian and archaeologist Leonard Clark, the area was named after Old Harry Head, near Portsmouth, England. Which story you want to believe is up to you. I usually choose the last one—but not always. Standing on the weather-beaten jetty—the fishing boats pulled up on the wooden slip—you'll see straight ahead the vast expanse of Plage de la

Exploring the caves and grottoes near La Bluff, Grande-Entrée. Grande Échouerie, stretching for over 10 km (6.2 mi.) to the most easterly point of land—Pointe-de-l'Est. Many islanders consider this beach—which forms the coastline of the Pointe-de-l'Est National Wildlife Reserve—the most wild and beautiful in the whole archipelago.

On your right, you'll see hundreds of strangely shaped

concrete blocks piled on top of each other. These are called dolosse and they're used as a breakwater and protection against erosion. The Magdalen Islands were the first place in Canada to test these structures, whose name is a South African word meaning the knuckle bone of a sheep—a reference, probably, to their unusual shape. You may wonder, as you look at the surrounding cliffs, why they were piled there as well. Good question! Apparently, when the harbour was built a larger breakwater was planned, but local authorities objected, so the unused dolosse were put there for possible future use.

Leaving the harbour, you'll climb over a small fence and continue to the tip of land jutting out to sea—Pointe Old-Harry. About 243 km (150 mi.) east of here is Newfoundland. The point is usually filled with Black-backed Gulls.

As you gaze onto the beaches, imagine thousands of walruses basking in the noon-day sun. In the seventeenth and eighteenth centuries Old-Harry was home to herds numbering in the tens of thousands. They were slaughtered by Europeans and Americans for their tusks and blubber and are now extinct in the Gulf.

The strange wind-in-a-bottle sound you can hear in the distance is a whistle buoy, situated not far off the coast. You should be able to spot it. These clever little devices operate under air pressure. As the buoy rides up a wave, a one-way valve opens to let air in; on its way down the other side of the wave the valve closes under pressure, forcing out a whistlelike sound.

Continuing along the route—just before you walk through the opening in the fence—back to the road, you'll see some caves in the small bay where cormorants and guillemots nest. They will have probably seen or heard your approach and begun to fly off to sea—a good time to use your binoculars.

After you cross the opening in the fence, continue alongside the road, heading towards the cliffs facing Seacow Bay. There's a visible path through the high grass. Don't go close to the edge of the cliffs—they are extremely dangerous. There are splendid views of Île Boudreau to the south.

When you reach a large post in the grass, you can turn around and head back to the starting point. The large pile of dolosse make an interesting subject for a photograph. Well ... I think so, anyway.

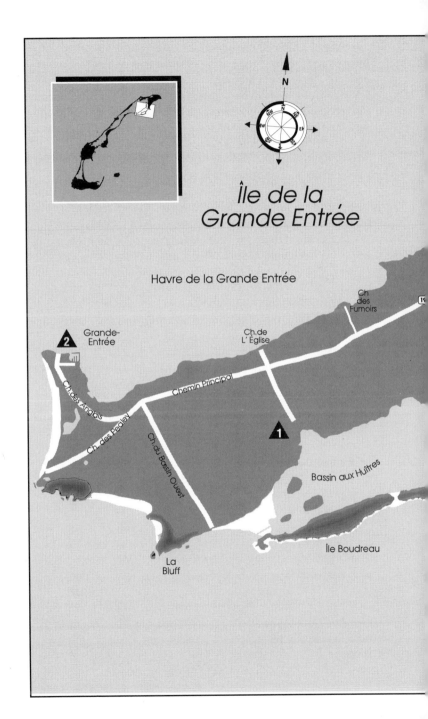

Île de la
Grande Entrée

Havre de la Grande Entrée

Ch. des Fumoirs

Grande-Entrée

Ch. de L' Eglise

Chemin Principal

Ch. des Anglais

Ch. des Pealey

Ch. du Bassin Ouest

Bassin aux Huîtres

La Bluff

Île Boudreau

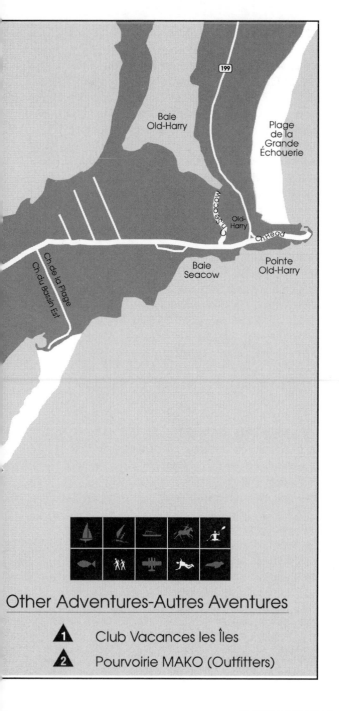

Other Adventures-Autres Aventures

1 Club Vacances les Îles

2 Pourvoirie MAKO (Outfitters)

Club vacances "Les Îles"

Underwater Cave Exploration Tours near Île Boudreau

The Club vacances "Les Îles" caters to adventurers and nature lovers. It offers various outdoor activities, including organized hikes in the Pointe-de-l'Est National Wildlife Reserve. One of the most exciting adventures offered is skin diving in the caves and cliffs near Île Boudreau.

You're provided with snorkels, flippers, a face mask, and an isothermal wet suit. When the boat reaches Île Boudreau, it's a thirty-minute walk to the caves. An experienced guide accompanies the group and demonstrates how to use the equipment and practise safety measures.

Pointe-de-l'Est Nature Walk

The Club vacances "Les Îles" offers a five- to six-hour hike along the Plage de la Grande Échouerie to Pointe-de-l'Est—the eastern extremity of the Magdalens. The hike, which is over 9 km (5.5 mi.) long, takes you along the outskirts of the Pointe-de-l'Est National Wildlife Reserve. You may see Piping Plovers. Grey seals, from the safety of the sea, often curiously follow your progress on the beach. At Pointe-de-l'Est, a cross was erected in 1969 in memory of a terrible maritime disaster—the sinking of the *Miracle*.

The *Miracle* carried immigrants between Liverpool, England and Québec City. On the evening of May 19, 1847, en route to Quebec with over four hundred passengers, it ran aground in a gale on a reef about a mile off Pointe-de-l'Est. The exact number who perished is unknown, but the survivors erected a huge cross at the mass grave—made from pieces of the ship.

How to get to Club vacances "Les Îles":

The Club vacances "Les Îles" is in Grande-Entrée. From the Tourist Bureau, turn right on 199 East or Chemin Principal and follow the signs for Grande-Entrée. It's about 55 km (35 mi.) and takes about thirty to forty minutes by car. When you see the blue sign—which you can't miss—for the Club vacances "Les Îles," you're just a few kilometres away.

For Further Information:

To inquire about prices, or joining one of the organized tours,

contact Club vacances "Les Îles," 377 Route 199, P.O. Box 59, Grande-Entrée, Îles-de-la-Madeleine, Quebec, GOB 1HO. Tel: (418) 985-2833. Fax: (418) 985-2226.

Pourvoirie MAKO (Outfitters)

Deep-Sea Shark Fishing

Mako sharks (a close relative of the Great White), Blue Sharks, and Spiny Sharks can all be found off the coast of the Magdalen Islands. But I mean far off the coast, so swimmers needn't be alarmed.

Captain Antoine Poirier and his experienced crew sail from the port of Grande-Entrée every day from July to October (weather permitting) to take adventuresome souls shark fishing. The prey can be up to 3.6 m (12 ft.) long and weigh 200 kg (450 lbs.). Mako sharks are said to be faster than the Great White and just as ferocious.

How to get to Pourvoirie MAKO:

It's in the port of Grande-Entrée. From the Tourist Bureau, turn right on 199 East or Chemin Principal and follow the signs for Grande-Entrée. It's 60 km (37 mi.) from the Tourist Bureau— about a forty-minute drive.

For Further Information:

For reservations and information contact Antoine Poirier, Captain, C.P. 121 Grande-Entrée, Îles-de-la-Madeleine, Quebec, GOB 1HO. Tel: (418) 985-2895.

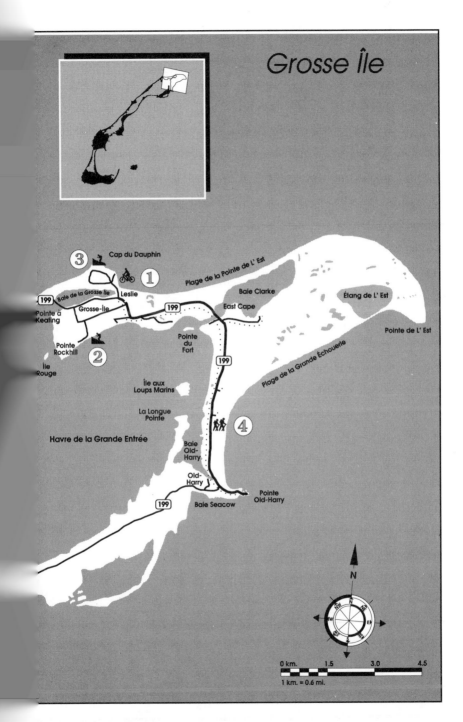

Grosse Île

Cap du Dauphin

3

1

Plage de la Pointe de L' Est

Leslie

Baie de la Grosse Île

199

Grosse-Île

199

Pointe à Keating

Pointe Rockhill

2

Île Rouge

Baie Clarke

East Cape

Étang de L' Est

Pointe de L' Est

Pointe du Fort

199

Plage de la Grande Échouerie

Île aux Loups Marins

La Longue Pointe

4

Havre de la Grande Entrée

Baie Old-Harry

Old-Harry

199

Baie Seacow

Pointe Old-Harry

N

0 km.   1.5   3.0   4.5
1 km. = 0.6 mi.

Grosse-Île to Pointe Old-Harry

Route Length:
The return trip is 20.4 km (12.6 mi.).

Approximate Time Required:
Cycling time is forty-five minutes to Pointe Old-Harry and the same for the return trip. But the scenic sites and nature walks can easily add another two hours.

Terrain:
The road's as flat as a pancake except for the small hill just past the post office at the start of the route.

Road Conditions:
There's a good paved road all the way to Pointe Old-Harry. Traffic is generally light on this stretch of Highway 199, but remember that drivers tend to speed up on the long straight stretches. Winds will generally be at your back, or just off to the side, blowing predominantly from the southwest.

What to Wear/Bring:
If you intend to do the two nature walks—Les Marais Salés and L'Échouerie—make sure to take a good mosquito repellent. You'll need it! Binoculars will come in handy to see Île Brion or the many species of birds that inhabit the Pointe-de-l'Est National Wildlife Reserve.

Precautions:
The cliffs at Cap du Dauphin, Pointe Old-Harry, and East Cape are extremely unstable. Stay well away from the edge. Mosquitoes can be a real nuisance at the nature walks of L'Échouerie and Les Marais Salés. Attention Frag'Îles recommends staying on existing paths to avoid damaging the fragile environment. Don't trample the Marram Grass on the dunes and avoid nesting areas of the Piping Plover on the Plage de la Grande Échouerie between May and August. This beach has a very dangerous undertow. Swim cautiously and stay near shore.

Difficulty:
A great trip for the whole family. No one should have any trouble finishing the ride.

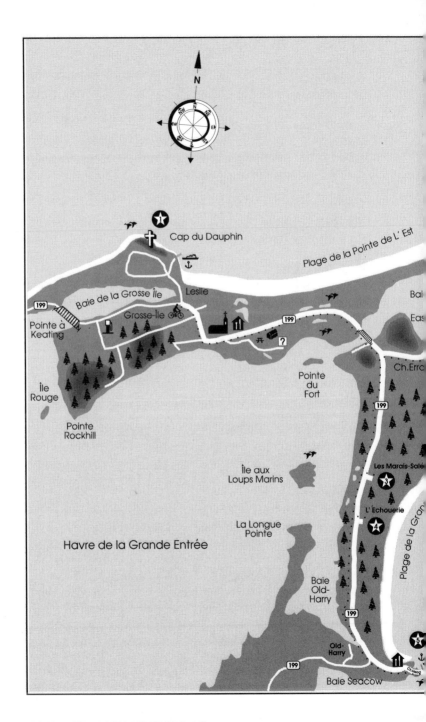

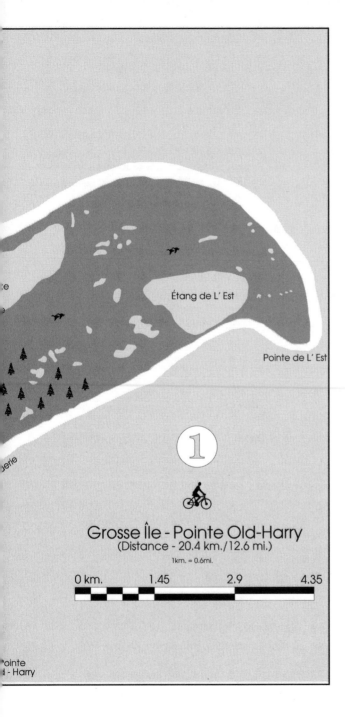

Étang de L' Est

Pointe de L' Est

1

Grosse Île - Pointe Old-Harry
(Distance - 20.4 km./12.6 mi.)

1km. = 0.6mi.

| 0 km. | 1.45 | 2.9 | 4.35 |

Facilities:

There are facilities along the route but mainly at the beginning and end of the trip, so get your supplies in Leslie or Pointe Old-Harry. If you don't have an air pump, the nearest gas station is about 1 km (.62 mi.) before Leslie on Highway 199.

Points of Interest:

1) View of Île Brion from the summit of Cap du Dauphin; 2) view of Baie Clarke and Pointe-de-l'Est National Wildlife Reserve from East Cape; 3) les Marais-Salés nature walk; 4) L'Échouerie nature walk; 5) harbour at Old-Harry.

Directions to Route Starting Point:

From the Tourist Bureau, turn right on Chemin Principal. Follow signs for 199 East, through Havre-aux-Maisons and Pointe-aux-Loups. Past Pointe-aux-Loups you'll pass the Mines Seleine on your right and the causeway leading into Grosse-Île. Just past the causeway, Highway 199 veers sharply to the right. At the intersection of 199 and Chemin North is the Leslie Post Office (number 427)—the start of this route. It's 43 km (26 mi.)—about a twenty-five-minute car ride from the Tourist Bureau.

Route Description:

0.0 km (0.0 mi.)   Welcome to Leslie—population 566. If you go inside the post office to mail a letter, don't be surprised to hear a Scottish or English accent instead of the French you've been hearing everywhere else. This village, and those of East Cape and Old-Harry, form one of the two anglophone communities in the Magdalen Islands. (The other, Île d'Entrée, or Entry Island, is an hour by ferry from Cap-aux-Meules.) About one thousand residents of the island are anglophones. Clarke, Keating, Dickson, and Quinn are the names you might hear along this route, instead of the more ususal Poirier, Richard, Thériault, and Turbide.

0.5 km (0.3 mi.)   Turn left from the post office onto 199 East and cycle up the small hill. At the top, there's a sharp turn to your left.

On a clear day, from the top of the hill you can see the uninhabited ecological reserve of Île Brion on your left. It's about 16 km (10 mi.) from the Grosse-Île harbour.

0.7 km (0.4 mi.)   The black-and-white Holy Trinity Church (number 541) is on your left.

It's a little soon to stop, but the beautiful stained-glass windows of this tiny church are worth it. They depict scenes of fishing—the main occupation of Magdalen Islanders.

2.8 km (1.7 mi.)   Continue straight on 199 East, passing through a wetland area with large ponds on either side of the road.

The Magdalen Islands are an important resting place for birds in their twice-yearly migrations. The small ponds on both sides are filled with many species of ducks. Where are those binoculars? The Black Duck, which looks black only from a distance—and is more widely known as the "Dusky Duck"—is common in this area. So are the Blue-winged Teals and the Greater Scaups. Rarer ducklike birds are the Horned Grebe, Red-Breasted Mergansers, and Goldeneyes. It's hard to tell them apart, so you might bring along a field guidebook.

4.0 km (2.5 mi.)   After crossing the small causeway, you'll see on your left a large blue sign for Pointe-de-l'Est National Wildlife Reserve (Les Marais-Salés—2.2 km, L'Échouerie—3.4 km). Turn left here onto Chemin Errol and continue to the end of road.

You are now in East Cape, which was the first anglophone settlement on the Magdalen Islands. Leave your bicycle at the edge of the road and climb to the 61-m (200-ft.) summit of East Cape for a magnificent view of the Point-de-l'Est National Wildlife Reserve, Baie Clarke, and the Plage de la Pointe de l'Est. This 684-ha (1,689-acre) wildlife area, owned and managed by the Canadian Wildlife Service, is the only such ecosystem in Quebec. You'll soon get an opportunity to hike into the reserve to observe the flora, fauna, and migratory bird life of this unique environment.

4.2 km (2.6 mi.)   Return to Highway 199 and turn left (east).

6.4 km(3.9 mi.)   Turn left at the small orange marker on the left-hand side of the road, and ride into the parking area for the Les Marais-Salés Nature Walk.

This 2-km (1.25-mi.) hike along a sandy path and boardwalk explores the ecosystem of the saltwater marsh, bog, dunes, and Stunted Forest. Descriptive panels and demonstrations explain

the environment. You'll learn about Sheep Laurel, Balsam Fir, Bayberry, Lichens, Common Junipers, Beach Grass, and Beach Heath. There are some insect-eating Pitcher Plants as well. But a word of warning—wear long clothes and use mosquito repellent. The Pitcher Plants try their best, but there just aren't enough of them.

6.4 km (3.9 mi.)   Turn left and continue east on Highway 199.

7.7 km (4.7 mi.)   Turn left at the next orange marker on the left-hand side of the road. This is the parking area for the L'Échouerie Nature Walk.

Another 2-km (1.25-mi.) hike along a path and boardwalk describes the roles that Stunted Dune Forests, fixed dunes, and active dunes play in maintaining levels of fresh ground water on the Magdalens and in supporting vegetation and bird life. The importance of Marram Grass (or beach grass) in holding dunes in place is also explained. Afterwards, you can wander onto the magnificent beach at La Plage de la Grande Échouerie. For a detailed description of the L'Échouerie route read page 57 (Hiking Route 4 - L'Échouerie).

9.3 km (5.7 mi.)   Highway 199 turns sharply right at the junction with Chemin Head. Turn left onto Chemin Head (sign is faded and hard to read) and continue to the harbour at Old-Harry.

10.2 km (6.3 mi.)   Stop at the harbour of Old-Harry.

Old-Harry, named after Old Harry Head near Portsmouth, England, was home to large herds of walruses in the 1700s. Americans and Europeans slaughtered them for their tusks and blubber and they are now extinct on these islands. Walk up to the outcropping of land known as Pointe Old-Harry and you can see the long beach called the Grande Échouerie. It stretches for over 10 km (6.2 mi.) to the most easterly tip of land—Pointe de l'Est. Below, you'll see the wooden pier of Old-Harry, held together by hundreds of odd-shaped blocks piled one on top of each other. These blocks, or dolosse, were first used in North America as a breakwater. The word "dolosse" is a South African term meaning the knuckle bone of a sheep. (See p. 33 for further explanation.) From Old-Harry Point you're only 243 km (150 mi.) from the

western tip of Newfoundland. As you circumnavigate this spit of land, you'll see a wide variety of birds including Black-backed Gulls, Double-crested Cormorants, and the distinctive guillemots.

20.4 km (12.6 mi.) Return to Highway 199 from Chemin Head and turn right on 199 West to return to starting point in Leslie.

If you have some extra time, turn right on Chemin North, just past the Leslie post office, make another right onto Chemin Shore and stop at the harbour.

Just to the left of the fish processing plant is an unpaved double-track road that will take you along the cliffs to the summit of Cap du Dauphin for an incredible view of Île Brion.

More than 16 km (10 mi.) from Grosse-Île, in the Gulf of St. Lawrence, the uninhabited Île Brion was discovered by Jacques Cartier in 1534. He was struck by the richness of its soil. Cartier named the island after the French admiral, Chabot de Brion.

In 1987 the Quebec government bought Île Brion and established a conservation and ecological reserve to protect the forest, vegetation, and more than 140 species of birds that nest there. The Brion Island Access and Protection Corporation allows pre-arranged overnight visits to the island. For more information on Old-Harry and Cap du Dauphin refer to page 52 (Climbing Route 3 - Cap du Dauphin) and page 29 (Climbing Route 3 - Pointe Old-Harry).

Pointe Rockhill

Route Length:
From Chemin Wide, where the route starts, to Pointe Rockhill, is 2.86 km (1.77 mi.).

Approximate Time Required:
This short hiking route should take just over half an hour each way.

Terrain:
The hike up Chemin Keating is along a red-dirt road that carves its way through a large forest of fir and white spruce. The slope is quite gentle, climbing to 76 m (250 ft.), descending to a clearing at sea level. The rest of the walk to Pointe Rockhill is along a shoreline of rocks and sand.

Difficulty:
The walk along Chemin Keating—up to the clearing at the abandoned house—can be done by anyone, including children. The rest of the way to the rocky outcrop facing Île Rouge, requires scrambling down a 15-m (50-ft.) sandstone slope to the sea and walking along a rocky coastline. Once you reach the clearing, you can decide whether to continue to Pointe Rockhill or just enjoy the fabulous views from where you are.

Precautions:
The forest alongside Chemin Keating is a great breeding place for mosquitoes. I strongly recommend mosquito repellent. The abandoned house at the end of Chemin Keating looks inviting—but it's ready to collapse, so resist the temptation. If you continue to Pointe Rockhill, be cautious on the 15-m (50-ft.) slope. It's best to do this hike at low tide, when the rocks along the shoreline are less slippery.

What to Wear/Bring:
As already mentioned, wear long pants, a long-sleeved shirt, socks, shoes, and a hat. And don't forget the mosquito repellent! Rubber sandals are good for walking along the shore, or you can go barefoot. Binoculars give you a better look at bird life and distant views out to sea.

When to Go:
If you want spectacular views of Dune du Nord, Île Rouge, and Havre de la Grande Entrée, pick a clear day. But I once hiked here on a foggy morning, and the still air and misty views were beautiful.

Points of Interest:
The bird life on Île Rouge and surrounding woodlands; views of Mines Seleine salt mine; spectacular views of Cap de l'Est, Havre de la Grande Entrée, Île aux Loups Marins, and the island of Grande Entrée.

Directions to Route Starting Point:
From the Tourist Bureau, turn right on Chemin Principal. Follow signs for 199 East, through Havre-aux-Maisons and Pointe-aux-Loups. Once you've passed the Mines Seleine salt mine and crossed the small causeway, you're on Grosse Île. Turn right on Chemin Rock Mountain and drive up the steep hill past the Hydro Quebec substation on your right. The road veers sharply left onto Chemin Wide, and after about 45 m (150 ft.) you'll see a red-dirt road on your right. This road (Chemin Keating), which is the start of the route, is not marked and is easy to miss. It's about a thirty-minute drive from the Tourist Bureau—42 km (26 mi.).

Île Rouge teems with a variety of aquatic birds.

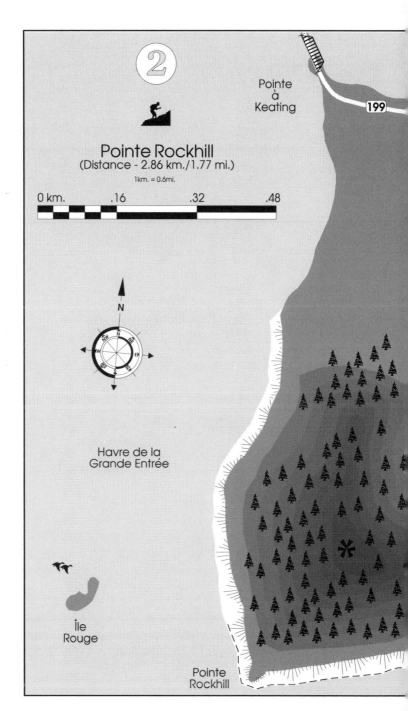

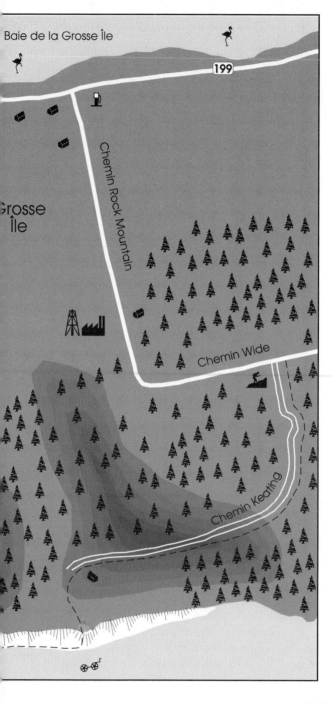

Route Description:

Once you've covered yourself with mosquito repellent you're ready to hike into the wonderful scent of fir and white spruce trees lining this route.

Follow Chemin Keating as it winds upwards towards the summit of Rock Mountain. In the silent forest you might hear the echoing call of the Long-eared Owl. Bird lovers can distinguish the calls of various species here—including the Olive-sided Flycatchers, Gray-cheeked Thrushes, Sharp-shinned Hawks, and Merlins. I still can't tell them apart. You might also catch a glimpse of a Great Blue Heron soaring overhead. A large colony of these graceful birds nests here, using the nearby lagoon as a source of food.

The forest you're walking through, and the one in Havre-Aubert, are the last mature forests on the Magdalen Islands. The heavy demand for wood, as well as generally poor conditions for forest development, has reduced forest coverage from 33 per cent of the islands to about 18 per cent. The environmental group Attention Frag'Îles carries on an educational campaign to teach the importance of forests to the Magdalens' fragile ecosystem. They work, as well, with the Quebec Department of Forests and federal government to develop ways of maintaining the islands' forests.

Eventually, Chemin Keating begins to descend towards the sea, and you'll emerge from the forest into a large grassy clearing facing the lagoon of Havre de la Grande Entrée.

Walk past the grey-shingled abandoned house towards the sea and look for the ravine, where you can scramble down to the seashore. A good way to spot the ravine is to look for the remnants of an old wagon sitting in the water a few metres offshore. The ravine's right in front of it. Be careful on your way down because the soil isn't very stable.

When you reach the shore turn right. To keep your shoes dry, it's best to go barefoot here or bring appropriate footwear. You can even leave your shoes here, and pick them up on the way back. The shoreline is dotted with large, loose stones that may be slippery. There are two rocky outcroppings to negotiate before you reach the sandy beach near Pointe Rockhill. As soon as you round the bend past the last rocky pinnacle, you'll see the tiny island of Île Rouge, teeming with aquatic birds.

Stop here, perch on a rocky ledge, and take in the wonderful

panorama. On your left you'll see the very tip of the Magdalen Islands—Grande-Entrée and the Île aux Loups Marins. On your right, the white Dune du Nord stretch like ribbons as far as the eye can see.

Also on your right, the Mines Seleine salt mine rises above the dunes. This salt mine was found accidentally in the early 1970s. The search for oil on the Magdalen Islands uncovered vast salt domes (or "mushrooms") 30-40 m (98-131 ft.) beneath the surface. The mine began operations on April 1, 1983. It's 300 m (984 ft.) deep; it produces more than 1.2 million metric tons (1.3 million tons) of road salt in eleven months and employs over two hundred people. Its projected capacity of over 450 million metric tons (over 495 million tons) would keep it open for fifty years. The salt is sold to Quebec, Newfoundland, and parts of the U.S. to put on icy roads. You might see the large ship that arrives weekly to transport the salt.

The beautiful archipelago that you're enjoying owes its existence to these salt domes, which over millenia have inched towards the surface, creating these islands.

Follow the route back to the starting point at Chemin Wide. Remember to pick up your shoes on the way back!

Cap du Dauphin

Route Length:
This circular route is 1.6 km (1.0 mi.) long.

Approximate Time Required:
You can hike this route in about thirty minutes. But if you stop to pick strawberries (in season), visit the pioneer cemetery and contemplate the breathtaking views from the summit; allow yourself an hour and a half.

Terrain:
This is an easy hike, with a clearly marked trail that follows an abandoned wagon track to the summit at 55 m (180 ft.).

Difficulty:
Anyone, including children, can easily do it. Because of the high, unprotected cliffs, watch the kids.

Savouring a well-deserved rest on the cliffs of Cap du Dauphin.

Precautions:
Stay well back from the edge of the cliffs, they're extremely unstable and eroding constantly. Within a few thousand years the Magdalen Islands may erode away completely! But in the meantime, remember that the winds can be very strong near the summit. Mosquitoes are generally not a problem here, but bring

repellent, because on those rare, windless days they get their own back—and yours.

What to Wear/Bring:
Whatever clothing and footwear you wish.

When to Go:
I suggest a clear day, so that you'll have an exceptional view of Île Brion and the whole panorama.

Points of Interest:
Views of the uninhabited ecological reserve of Île Brion; Baie de la Grosse Île; Plage de la Pointe de l'Est; and Dune du Nord. Pioneer English cemetery dating back to 1800s.

Directions to Route Starting Point:
From the Tourist Bureau, turn right on Chemin Principal. Follow 199 East, through Havre-aux-Maisons, Pointe-aux-Loups and onto Grosse-Île. On Grosse-Île, turn left on Chemin North and continue to Chemin Shore. Turn right on Chemin Shore and follow the road to the harbour. It's about a thirty-five minute drive—44 km (27 mi.).

Route Description:
Although Cap du Dauphin means "Dolphin Cape" in English, I don't think you'll see any on your hike. I haven't yet.

Before heading out, visit the picturesque harbour with its brightly painted fishing boats nestled alongside the wharf. *L'Île de Brion* sails from here to the uninhabited ecological reserve of Île Brion—a 16 km (10 mi.) trip.

Your route starts just behind the large warehouse-type building. It's the Grosse-Île fish processing plant. You can peek inside to see how fish such as Mackerel are processed.

From the fish plant, head towards the cliffs until you find the double-track path.

Follow the path as it winds up Cap du Dauphin past the cemetery. Keep at least 9 m (30 ft.) from the edge of these cliffs. They're high and unstable.

Within ten or fifteen minutes you'll reach the cross atop Cap du Dauphin. Gaze out to the north from here and you should be able to make out Île Brion.

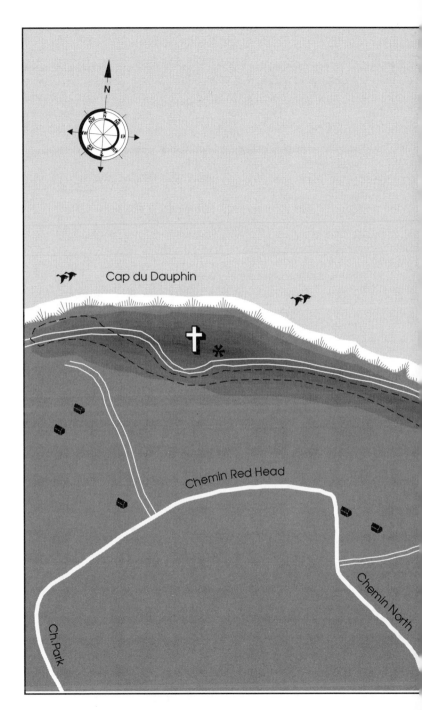

Cap du Dauphin

Chemin Red Head

Chemin North

Ch. Park

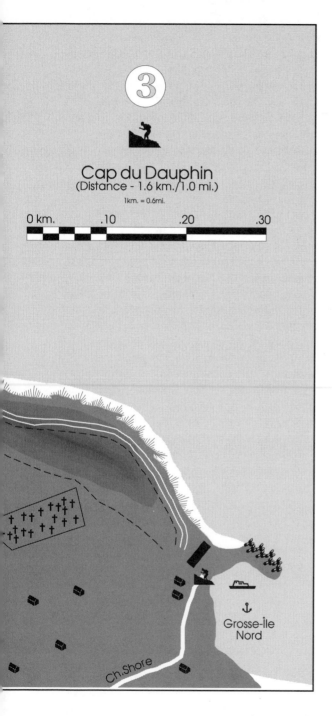

③

Cap du Dauphin
(Distance - 1.6 km./1.0 mi.)

1km. = 0.6mi.

0 km.   .10   .20   .30

Grosse-Île
Nord

Ch.shore

Île Brion, about 16 km (10 mi.) off Grosse-Île, was discovered in 1534 by Jacques Cartier who stopped there overnight to replenish his supplies. He was struck by the beauty of the landscape and the richness of the soil, forest, and wildlife. It was here that Cartier first saw huge herds of walruses. He likened the enormous, tusked mammals to elephants in water. Cartier named the island Île de Brion after his friend and patron Philippe de Chabot, Seigneur de Brion—the Grand Admiral of France.

Until the beginning of the 1970s the island was inhabited on a seasonal basis—mainly by Basque fisherman during the fishing season. In 1987 the Government of Quebec bought the island to establish a conservation and ecological reserve. The whole island and its more than 140 species of birds are now protected.

With binoculars, you can see the lighthouse and the Dingwell house at the western tip of the island, where at least twenty people lived. Île Brion is about 7.5 km (4.5 mi.) long.

Facing southwards, you'll have a sweeping view of the small inland body of water—Baie de la Grosse Île—and the Dune du Nord, whose more than 20 km (12.4 mi.) of unspoiled sandy beaches extend to Pointe-aux-Loups.

From the summit, follow the path down to a large grassy field that's usually overflowing with field strawberries during the last two weeks of July. Further on is the little cemetery, where generations of the English/Scottish community—such as the Clarkes, Keatings, and Quinns—are buried. Some of the weathered gravestones, with haunting epitaphs, date back to the 1800s. Please be respectful of the area which is on private land.

Pointe-de-l'Est (l'Échouerie)

Route Length:
The return trip to the Plage de la Grande Échouerie is 2 km (1.24 mi.).

Approximate Time Required:
It takes about thirty minutes to reach the beach at the Plage de la Grande Échouerie if you read all the panels along the way and fifteen minutes to return to the parking area. But if you choose to linger at the magnificent white sand beach of Plage de la Grande Échouerie, you may completely lose track of time.

Terrain:
This easy, self-guiding nature trail is clearly marked; it's first a sandy path and then a boardwalk. Signs along the way describe and show examples of rare and varied vegetation in the area.

Difficulty:
An easy walk for the whole family—but you'll be swarmed by mosquitoes.

Precautions:
Except for the dangerous undertow at the Plage de la Grande Échouerie, the mosquitoes are the only other thing to worry about. Stay on the network of paths to avoid damaging this fragile environment. Several species of endangered plants grow here, such as the Woody Hudsonia *(Hudsonie tomenteuse)* and Broom Crowberry *(Corema conradii)*. When you walk on the beach, avoid the nesting grounds of the Piping Plover—an endangered species—and don't trample the beach grass growing on the dunes. The grass literally helps hold the dunes together.

What to Wear/Bring:
Mosquito repellent, mosquito repellent, and more mosquito repellent! From the second you get out of the car you'll become a walking feast for these hungry critters. Without protection you won't enjoy stopping to read about the various flora and fauna in this fascinating ecosystem. Wear long pants, a long-sleeved shirt, socks, and a hat for extra protection. Bring binoculars if you're a birdwatcher—and a bathing suit.

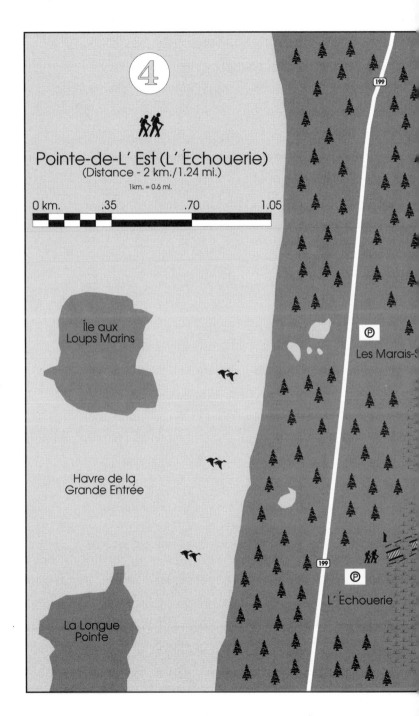

④

Pointe-de-L' Est (L' Échouerie)
(Distance - 2 km./1.24 mi.)

1km. = 0.6 ml.

0 km.   .35   .70   1.05

Île aux
Loups Marins

Les Marais-S

Havre de la
Grande Entrée

199

L' Échouerie

La Longue
Pointe

199

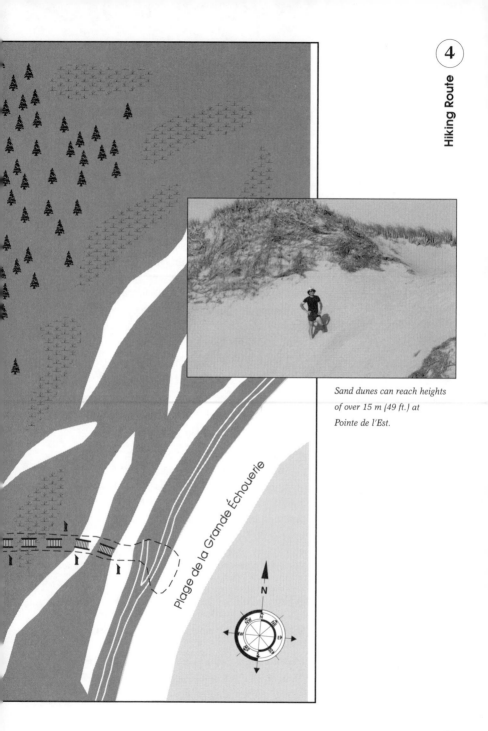

*Sand dunes can reach heights
of over 15 m (49 ft.) at
Pointe de l'Est.*

Plage de la Grande Échouerie

N

When to Go:
Any time of day is fine, but the bugs are worse in the early morning and late evening.

Points of Interest:
I hope my mosquito warning hasn't scared you off this route, because the wetlands are fascinating. The lunarlike landscape, teeming with life, shouldn't be missed. You'll see the carnivorous Pitcher Plant, the dunes and beaches of the Plage de la Grande Échouerie, and a large variety of migratory birds.

Directions to Route Starting Point:
From the Tourist Bureau, turn right on Chemin Principal and take 199 East through Havre-aux-Maisons, Pointe-aux-Loups, and Grosse-Île. After crossing a small bridge at East Cape, you'll see a large blue sign saying that the L'Échouerie walk is 3.4 km (2.1 mi.) ahead. You'll first pass the Les Marais-Salés walk, which is identified only by a very small, circular orange marker. The second orange marker on your left—which can easily be missed—marks the beginning of the l'Échouerie walk. Turn left into the parking area. From the Tourist Bureau to here is 50 km (31 mi.)—about thirty minutes by car.

Route Description:
If you don't know the difference between dunes, lagoons, moors, salt meadows, marshes, saltwater ponds, Balsam fir, White Spruce, Cowberry, Common Juniper, Labrador Tea, Sweet Gale, and Sheep Laurel, you certainly will after this 2-km (1.24-mi.) hike. Descriptive panels and demonstrations interpret the ecology. This is one small section of the 684-ha (1,690-acre) Pointe-de-l'Est National Wildlife Reserve.

Owned and managed by Environment Canada's Canadian Wildlife Service, the area is the only example, in Quebec, of such an ecosystem.

The route starts to the left of the parking lot. Just follow the sandy path and then the boardwalk right to the end. Interpretive panels along the way describe examples of the vegetation found here.

The first type of vegetation described is the Stunted Dune Forest. You'll see Balsam Fir, White Spruce, Labrador Tea, Sweet Gale, and Sheep Laurel. The main ecological role of this forest is

to stabilize the shifting dunes, but don't tell that to the songbirds that live here: the Ruby-crowned Kinglet, Tennessee Warbler, Red-breasted Nuthatch, White-throated and Savannah sparrows— amongst others. A guidebook will help.

Further along you enter a second area—the Fixed Dune, characterized by the crowberry moor (a bog), Cowberry, Common Juniper, Common Bearberry and Three-toothed Cinquefoil. The Cowberry (or mountain cranberry), Common Juniper, and Bearberry all have various medicinal uses. Unless you're a field botanist don't sample any of the plants or berries. Some are poisonous. Animals in this area include deer mice, meadow voles, red squirrels, and red foxes. You'll be happy to know the carnivorous Pitcher Plant relishes mosquitoes.

After climbing a long flight of stairs, you come to a third ecological area—the Active Dunes. Dunes are vital to the ecosystem of the Magdalen Islands. They prevent the sea from flooding the lowlands and contaminating fresh ground water sources. Each island depends on its supply of ground water—the resource that is often strained at the height of the tourist season.

Marram Grass, or beach grass as it is sometimes called, helps to keep dunes intact. Its long rhizomes, or stems, penetrate deep into the dunes, which hold sand in place when the wind blows. Marram Grass is very susceptible to trampling—by hikers, or riders of all-terrain vehicles. When a plant is crushed, its root system dies. If this "mesh" of roots that holds the sand in place is destroyed, the dunes, eventually, will blow away. These grasses, also called "dune hay" were once harvested for livestock feed.

As you walk towards the Plage de la Grande Échouerie remember the importance of Marram Grass to this ecosystem. Take the sandy path between the dunes, where no marram grass grows.

When you reach the Plage de la Grande Échouerie you can turn around in your tracks or sit down and spend a few hours not thinking about the return trip. Tough choice!

When you do head back along the interpretive trail, consider these properties of some of the plants you've seen: Labrador Tea is used as a cold remedy—an expectorant; Sweet Gale leaves are used to reduce fever and act as a mosquito repellent (now you tell us!); Bearberry stems and leaves are used against headaches and as an antibacterial treatment for urinary tract disorders; Cowberry juice is used to treat cystitis; and juniper is used against colds, acne, eczema, and rheumatism.

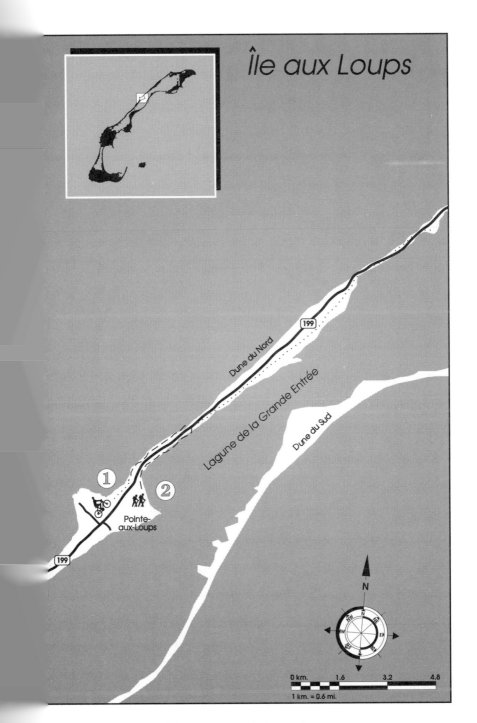

Île aux Loups

199

Dune du Nord

Lagune de la Grande Entrée

Dune du Sud

① ②

Pointe-
aux-Loups

199

N

0 km.   1.6   3.2   4.8
1 km. = 0.6 mi.

Île aux Loups to Mines Seleine

Route Length:
The return-trip distance for this cycling route is 32.4 km (20 mi.).

Approximate Time Required:
Since the wind will probably be at your back on your way north, it will take a seemingly effortless hour to reach the Mines Seleine. Getting back to Île aux Loups won't be nearly as easy. You'll be battling strong headwinds. It should take about an hour and a half to get back.

Terrain:
The road from Île aux Loups to the Mines Seleine is as straight as an arrow. Don't worry about hills. The elevation for the entire distance is 0 metres above sea level. That's because, on this stretch of Highway 199, the sea is on both sides of the road.

Road Conditions:
The route is paved, with a gravel shoulder. Drivers, especially truckers, drive quite fast along here, but traffic is light. Crosswinds sometimes occur, and large trucks passing by can create a suctionlike effect, pulling you into the middle of the road. Horseflies can be a nuisance. They'll follow you for miles!

What to Wear/Bring:
You might want to go clam digging in the lagoon, but that means packing a pail and shovel—just a thought. You should have binoculars to observe the bird life at Lac Goose and Grand Étang.

Precautions:
The cliffs at Anse de l'Est and Pointe du Cap, which are over 15 m (50 ft.) high can crumble easily beneath your weight. Keep a safe distance from the edge. The dunes and the Marram Grass in this area are considered to be very fragile. Wherever possible, use existing paths to cross the dunes, and be careful not to trample the Marram Grass. Two rare and endangered birds, the Piping Plover and the Horned Grebe, are found in this area and should not be disturbed. Use your binoculars—especially in nesting season. If you intend to swim at Plage de la Dune du Nord, stay close to the shore. The currents, particularly on windy days, can be very dangerous.

Difficulty:

You'll need a bit of stamina and determination to conquer the strong headwinds on your way back to Île aux Loups. When I cycled this route, the winds were so fierce that it seemed as though I spent the whole time facing the pavement. By the end, I knew exactly how many white highway lines were painted on the road—963 stripes. Let me know if you count a different number!

Facilities:

There are no facilities along this route except for the grocery store and snack bar at Île aux Loups. Make sure you fill your water bottles and stock up on high-energy munchies.

Cycling into Pointe-aux-Loups.

Points of Interest:

1) Cliffs and harbour at Pointe du Cap and Anse de L'Est; 2) view of Dune du Sud and Lagune de la Grande Entrée from Chemin du Quai Sud harbour; 3) deserted beaches and dunes of Plage de la Dune du Nord; 4) Horned Grebes and Snowy Owls at Lac Goose; 5) salt mine operation of Mines Seleine.

Directions to Route Starting Point:

From the Tourist Bureau, turn right on Chemin Principal. Follow signs for 199 East, which takes you through Havre-aux-Maisons and into Pointe-aux-Loups. In Pointe-aux-Loups, stop at the church on your left. It's 24 km (14.9 mi.)—fifteen minutes by car.

Route Description:

Île aux Loups, or Wolf Island, is a fishing community of just over two hundred residents. It lies like a shimmering mirage between the vast sandy arms of Dune du Nord. There's not a fax to be found!

0.0 km (0.0 mi.)   From the church, turn right onto 199 West, then right again onto Chemin du Quai Nord.

0.64 km (0.37 mi.)   Arrive at the small fishing port of Île aux Loups.

Leave your bicycle at the harbour and take the path just to the right of a small Hydro Quebec generator station. In a few minutes, when you've reached the top of Pointe du Cap, you'll have a spectacular view of the Dune du Nord—two golden rivers of sand flowing north and south. From here, the closest landfall is the Gaspé Peninsula, just over 200 km (124 mi.) away.

Gales, thick fog, dangerous reefs, and tricky currents make the Dune du Nord a sailor's nightmare. More than fifty ships have gone down along its 40 km (25 mi.) of coastline. Names such as *Protector, Warrior, Watchful,* and the *Wasp* couldn't keep them from a watery grave. November 28, 1871, was a bone-chilling morning. The wind howled. The sky was dark with menacing clouds. A blanket of fog enshrouded Île aux Loups and the Dune du Nord. Suddenly, the cargo ship *Wasp* emerged from the fog and slammed onto the dunes, spilling its cargo of wheat and crew of eleven into the icy waters. Augustin Lebourdais—who eventually became the first Morse telegrapher on the Magdalen Islands—was the sole survivor.

Continue north along the 15-m (50-ft.) cliffs of Pointe du Cap. You can see guillemots and cormorants nesting in the rocky pinnacles, but as always, stay well back from the cliff edge—it's not solid.

1.28 km (.76 mi.)   Return to the port and cycle back along Chemin du Quai Nord. Cross Highway 199 and continue along Chemin du Quai Sud to its end.

1.92 km (1.19 mi.)   Arrive at the Harbour of Chemin du Quai Sud.

Looking north from the harbour you see the very tip of the Magdalen Islands—Grande Entrée—rising just above the horizon. Directly ahead, the Dune du Sud and the Lagune de la Grande

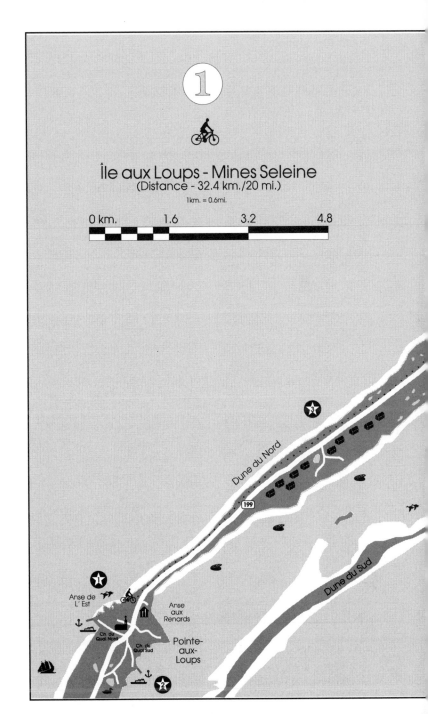

① 🚴

Île aux Loups - Mines Seleine
(Distance - 32.4 km./20 mi.)

1km. = 0.6mi.

| 0 km. | 1.6 | 3.2 | 4.8 |

Dune du Nord

199

Dune du Sud

Anse de
L' Est

Anse
aux
Renards

Ch. du
Quai Nord

Ch. du
Quai Sud

Pointe-
aux-
Loups

Entrée protect Pointe-aux-Loups from the full force of the sea. It's an ecological safety-zone for the birds and marine life that inhabit the lagoon. On a clear day, looking south, you might see the towering wind-generator on Dune du Sud. It looks like an upside-down eggbeater. In 1977, the Magdalen Islands were chosen as the site of the world's largest vertical-axis wind turbine. It was invented in France by Felix Darrieus, and further developed in Canada, in the 1960s. Constant winds of up to 40 km/hour (25 mph) would enable it to generate 200 kw of power—sufficent to provide electricity to thirty homes—more cheaply than the diesel-generated electricity plant built in 1953. In 1978 the entire structure fell down. (Maybe it was too windy!) It was rebuilt in 1981. In the fifteen years that I've been going to the islands, I have only seen the eggbeater in action once. To this date it remains in the experimental stages.

2.5 km (1.55 mi.) Cycle back along Chemin du Quai Sud to Highway 199. Turn right onto 199 East.

5.4 km (3.34 mi.) Stop at the cluster of chalets built along the sand dunes—on your right.

Leave your bicycle and take the path on the right to the Lagune de la Grande Entrée. It's a ten to fifteen minute walk. The lagoon is one of three on the islands.

As well as being a warmer place to swim, lagoons play a vital role by providing a habitat that supports various species of birds and fish. This is the place for clam digging. It's best when the water's calm. And you'll need that pail and shovel—which you've probably forgotten. But should you be prepared, just look for small holes in the sand and dig 18-20 cm (7-8 in.) beneath them to unearth a delectable treasure. Don't dig with your hands; the shells' sharp edges can cut your fingers.

When you walk back to Highway 199, cross the road and take the sandy path over the dunes on the other side—to the beaches of Dune du Nord. The turquoise water looks inviting, but it's ususally toe-numbing. It's a perfect place to build a sand castle, walk along the deserted beach, or search for buried treasure. These giant sand dunes comprise 60 per cent of the Magdalens' coastal area and one-third of the land mass. Always remember their fragility—particularly the Marram Grass which grows on top. Try not to trample the grass and follow existing breaches or

breaks in the dune. If you destroy the Marram Grass, which sta-
bilizes the sand, the shifting dunes may eventually spread over
the islands.

11.0 km (6.82 mi.) Continue on 199 East until you see two large
lakes on your right—Lac Goose and Grand Étang. Stop here.

Whether you're an ornithologist (a bird lover) or you can't tell
a Great Blue Heron from a swallow, you should stop here to see
the bird life that inhabits the freshwater marshes. Follow the dirt
road that runs parallel to Highway 199 towards the Lagune de la
Grande Entrée. With the aid of binoculars and a field guide on
birds you may spot the rare Horned Grebe that inhabits the area.
It has a conspicuous orange plume around it's ears and a sharp
bill. But don't confuse the Horned Grebe with the Pied-billed
Grebe, the most common grebe in eastern North America. It
confuses, I admit.

If you're particularly lucky you'll see a Snowy Owl. It's easy
to recognize this rare and beautiful pure white bird—but look on
the ground, because it doesn't sit in trees.

16.2 km (10.0 mi.) Stop at the Mines Seleine.

Looking out of place amidst the sea and sand dunes, the vast
complex of the Mines Seleine rises abruptly from the surrounding
landscape. And what you see is only the tip of the salt mines—so
to speak. About 300 m (984 ft.) below the surface, a labyrinth of
tunnels and shafts extends over 1,600 m (1 mi.)—half is under the
Dune du Nord and half under the sea. The mine opened on April
1, 1983. It produces more than 1.2 million metric tons (1.3 million tons) of road salt in eleven months. Its estimated capacity of
450 million metric tons would keep it going for fifty years. More
than two hundred people work here. You might catch a glimpse
of the ship that arrives regularly to transport the salt to Quebec,
Newfoundland, and the United States. A channel 10.8 km (7 mi.)
long and 100 m (328 ft.) wide was dug in the Lagune de La
Grande Entrée to allow the ship safe passage. If you're curious
about the mines, go into the office and ask about the operations.
The next time you see a truck salting the road, remember that the
salt probably came from the Magdalen Islands.

32.4 km (20 mi.) Turn around and return to Île aux Loups on
199 West.

(2)

Île aux Loups to Dune du Nord

Route Length:
This hike is 6 km (3.7 mi.) long, but because it's all along the beach, you may feel as though you've walked twice that distance when you're finished.

Approximate Time Required:
It takes about three to four hours to complete this hike, allowing time for clam digging and swimming.

Terrain:
The route follows the tranquil eastern shore of Lagune de la Grande Entrée, then the wild, surf-pounded beaches of Dune du Nord on the west side. If you feel you're sinking to the knees with each step, walk as close to the water as possible. The sand's firmer there.

Difficulty:
A great hike for the whole family. Kids will love the clam digging.

Precautions:
The fragile sand dunes are a vital component of the Magdalen Islands ecosystem. When you're walking across them, or along the beach, don't trample the Marram Grass, which helps to stabilize the shifting sand. Try to follow existing paths atop the dunes. If you want to swim at Dune du Nord, stay close to shore. There are strong currents and an undertow . Once in a while you may feel the stinging bite of windblown sand.

What to Wear/Bring:
Shorts (bathing suit underneath), T-shirt, and sandals. I also recommend a good sun screen because the dunes and lagoons intensify the sun's rays. Bring pail and shovel for clam digging—and some bottled water. It's like the desert here—"water water everywhere, but not a drop to drink."

When to Go:
Any time—but if you want to dig for clams find out when low tide is (from the Tourist Bureau) and go then.

Points of Interest:

Clam digging in Lagune de la Grande Entrée; views of Dune du Sud and Grande Entrée; sand dunes and deserted white beaches of Dune du Nord—great swimming.

Directions to Route Starting Point:

From the Tourist Bureau, turn right on Chemin Principal. Follow signs for 199 East, through Havre-aux-Maisons and then Pointe-aux-Loups. Continue through the village, passing the church and the Casse-croûte - La Pointe, a small snack bar that sells hot dogs and fries. A few hundred metres further, on your left, you'll see a green welcome sign—À Bientôt. Park here, on the gravel shoulder, and cross Highway 199 to the lagoon side (east side). It's 25 km (15.5 mi.) from the Tourist Bureau—fifteen minutes by car.

Route Description:

A boundless blue sky, seemingly endless sand dunes and a shimmering ocean all converge here at Pointe-aux-Loups—a tiny green oasis amidst sea and sand.

Cross Highway 199 to the east side and walk north on the sandy shoreline of Lagune de la Grande Entrée. You should be able to make out the tip of the islands—Grande Entrée, and, further east, the Dune du Sud. The lagoon that this route follows is one of three on the Magdalen Islands—Lagune du Havre aux Basques and Lagune du Havre aux Maisons are further south.

Lagoons are formed when parallel sand dunes enclose a body of water leaving a channel open to the sea. Because they're protected from waves and winds, they warm up much faster than the surrounding sea and can support a host of marine and bird life.

Clams love lagoons. If you're here at low tide and you brought a pail and shovel, I can teach you to dig for your dinner. Look for small holes, or bubbles of water coming from the sand. Dig 18-20 cm (7-8 in.) under the hole and you'll have a delicious clam to take home and steam. That's all there is to it! Don't dig with your hands; you can get some nasty cuts from the shells' sharp edges.

A more commercially important habitat supported by the lagoons is that of the Blue Mussels. Mussel farming is business here. "Collectors" are placed in lagoons in early June. Young mussels affix themselves and begin to grow in colonies. In late September, the colonies are removed from the collectors and

②

Île aux Loups - Dune du Nord
(Distance - 6 km./3.7 mi.)

1km. = 0.6mi.

0 km.   1   2   3

Ragged cliffs at Pointe du Cap.

Dune du Nord

Anse de L' Est

Pointe du Cap

Anse aux Renards

Ch.du Quai Nord

Chemin Leblanc

Pointe-aux-Loups

199

Ch. du Quai Sud

Chemin Arseneau

Anse aux Canards

Lac aux Canards

199

gune de la Grande Entrée

Dune du Sud

N

Dune du Nord flows endlessly north and south.

placed on nets, where they continue growing. They're harvested when they reach market size—5 cm (2 in.).

Continue north along the lagoon passing twenty-four telephone poles (it's the best way to measure the distance), or about 2.75 km (1.7 mi.). About here you should see a small rowboat anchored in the lagoon. Turn left at this point and cross the dunes, taking care not to trample the Marram Grass.

When you reach Highway 199, look for a telephone pole on the west side with an orange band around it. Cross the road and climb the dunes to the Plage de la Dune du Nord, following the sandy path. Sand dunes comprise 60 per cent of the Magdalen Islands' coast and one-third of their land mass. The islands have 300 km (189 mi.) of beaches—a great trick for an area only about 100 km (62 mi.) from tip to tip. It's the three lagoons that give the extra beach mileage. At first glance, the dunes may appear lifeless, but if you look closely, you'll see all kinds of creatures—including beetles, ants, horseflies, and sand fleas—scurrying across the sand and making their way through the prickly Marram Grass.

The dunes reach heights of over 9 m (30 ft.), and it's a bit of a struggle up the sandy path. As you climb, you'll hear the surf crashing against the shore. When you crest the last dune, golden sand stretches to the horizon—bordered by a bottle-green sea.

Go left, or south, along the beach. In the distance you can make out the cliffs of Anse de l'Est and Pointe du Cap on Île aux Loups. As on any good beach, the sea brings beautiful shells and unusual artifacts ashore. You can watch sandpipers feeding at the edge of the waves, or simply listen to the sand crunching beneath your feet.

Just past the rocky pier turn left, walk back to Highway 199 then back to your starting point.

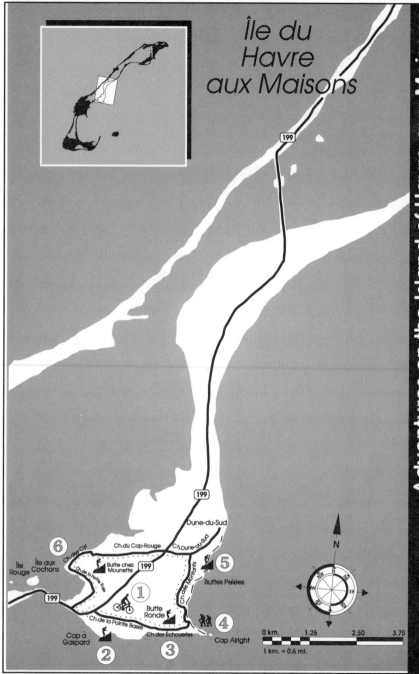

Île du
Havre
aux Maisons

199

199

Dune-du-Sud

Ch.du Cap-Rouge

Ch.Dune-du-Sud

6

Ch.des Oir

Butte chez Mounette

199

5

Île Rouge

Île aux Cochans

Ch.de la Petite Baie

1

Ch.des Montants

Buttes Pelées

199

Butte Ronde

Cap à Gaspard

Ch.de la Pointe Basse

2

Ch.des Échoueries

3

Cap Alright

4

N

0 km.   1.25   2.50   3.75

1 km. = 0.6 mi.

Cycling Route

Havre aux Maisons

Route Length:
This cycling route is 23 km (14.3 mi.) long.

Approximate Time Required:
Pedalling-time is about two hours, but if you stop at all the scenic sites along the way, tack on at least two more hours.

Terrain:
The good news is that most of the route is level. Chemin de la Pointe-Basse, Chemin des Échoueries, Chemin du Cap-Rouge, and Chemin de la Petite-Baie are all relatively flat roads. The bad news is that Chemin des Montants, or Mountain Road, is as steep and twisty as its name suggests. It's work, although the summit of Buttes Pelées doesn't sound that high—110 m (360 ft.). There's only one other steep ascent—the left turn from Chemin de la Dune du Sud onto 199 West, heading towards La Méduse. But it's more gradual and shorter than Chemin des Montants. The reward for struggling up both these "hills" is fabulous, awe inspiring vistas—and long, long descents!

Road Conditions:
Most of this ride meanders through rural countryside, along quiet, paved roads with little or no traffic—except a cow here and there. Some sections—including Chemin des Échoueries, Chemin des Montants, Chemin des Cyr, and Chemin de la Petite-Baie—are along unpaved roads better-suited to mountain bikes. Motorists generally drive faster on Highway 199, the main road on the archipelago. When you're on 199, you should cycle more cautiously and stay on to the right-hand side of the road.

What to Wear/Bring:
A bathing suit, in case you want to swim at Dune du Sud. There are plenty of facilities on this route so you won't need to carry much extra. Bring mosquito repellent if you want to hike to the top of Butte Ronde or Butte chez Mounette. Mosquitoes can be a pain in the butt on the butte. No apologies offered.

Precautions:
The cliffs at Buttes Pelées, Cap à Gaspard, and Cap Alright are

very unstable and subject to strong, gusting winds. Stay at least 9 m (30 ft.) from the edge. The route up Buttes Pelées and Butte Ronde has sections where you'll climb beside a barbed wire fence that's sometimes electrified with a very low current. It's not enough "juice" to hurt you, but it discourages cows from climbing to the top. Hungry mosquitoes often line the trail to the summit of Butte chez Mounette and Butte Ronde.

Suitability:

Except for the gruelling push to the top of Buttes Pelées, this route is a piece of cake, and no one should have much difficulty in completing the circuit. Don't be embarrassed if you have to get off your bicycle on Chemin des Montants and push it to the top. You'll be in good company. I, and lots of others, chose to dismount. Then again, some of you may relish the challenge of pedalling to the summit. More power to you!

Facilities:

You won't go hungry or thirsty along this route.

Points of interest:

1) Au Vieux Couvent convent and panoramic views from Cap à Gaspard; 2) old smokehouses and boat building shop in the tiny fishing port of Pointe-Basse; 3) lighthouse, cliff formations, and bird life at Cap Alright. Vistas from Butte Ronde; 4) volcanic peaks of Buttes Pelées; 5) sculpted cliffs and beaches of Dune du Sud; 6) glassblowing studio of La Méduse; 7) art exhibitions at Galerie d'Art Point-Sud; 8) 360-degree views from Butte chez Mounette.

Directions to Route Starting Point:

From the Tourist Bureau, turn right on Chemin Principal. Follow signs for 199 East, cross a green bridge into Havre-aux-Maisons. On your right, just past the Irving gas station, you'll see a three-storey stone building and a sign for Au Vieux Couvent Hotel. The route starts at the hotel's parking lot. From the Tourist Bureau, it's about 5 km (3mi.) to here—five minutes by car.

Route Description:

0.0 km (0.0 mi.)   Cycle down the dirt road from the Au Vieux Couvent Hotel and turn right onto Highway 199 East.

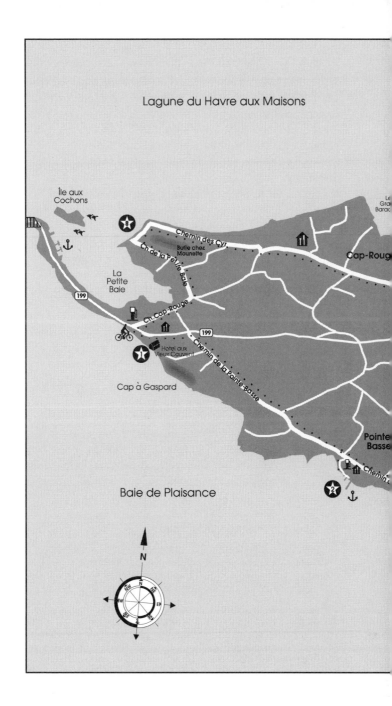

Lagune du Havre aux Maisons

Île aux
Cochons

La
Petite
Baie

199

Chemin des Cyr

Butte chez
Mounette

Ch. de la Petite Baie

Cap-Roug

Ch. Cap-Rouge

199

Chemin de la Pointe Basse

Hôtel aux
Vieux Couvent

Cap à Gaspard

Le
Gra
Barac

Pointe
Basse

Chemin

Baie de Plaisance

N

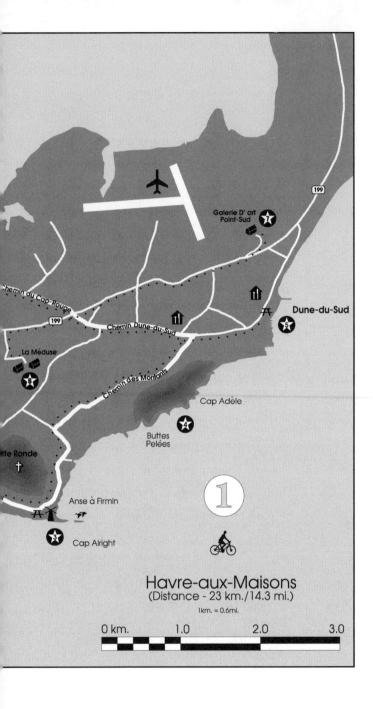

Galerie D' art
Point-Sud

199

Dune-du-Sud

Chemin du Cap-Rouge

199

Chemin Dune-du-Sud

La Méduse

Chemin des Montants

Cap Adèle

Buttes
Pelées

te Ronde

Anse à Firmin

Cap Alright

1

Havre-aux-Maisons
(Distance - 23 km./14.3 mi.)

1km. = 0.6mi.

0 km.   1.0   2.0   3.0

Before setting out, sit down on the hotel's sunny terrace—just a stone's throw from the sea—order yourself a Moules Alfredo avec frites (no, I won't translate that for you!) with a glass of white wine, and imagine, for a moment, the history of this converted convent school. Built in 1917-18 by the nuns of the Order of Notre-Dame des Flots, it's still the highest cut-stone structure on the Magdalens. La Moulière—a restaurant near the entrance—was once the chapel. The ten guest rooms upstairs were classrooms, and the "resto-bar" and terrace were the Mother Superior's sleeping quarters. Prayer and meditation have given way to an all-night jazz bar—at Chez Gaspard. What would the Mother Superior think!

Don't miss the chance to climb the heights of Cap à Gaspard—just behind the hotel—for indescribable views of the surrounding area. (A full description of Climbing Route 2 - Cap à Gaspard is on page 86.)

0.5 km (0.3 mi.)   Just up the road from Au Vieux Couvent, turn right onto Chemin de la Pointe-Basse.

Although I said earlier that Chemin de la Pointe-Basse is relatively flat, I forgot to mention the short incline you're now facing—.7 km (.4 mi.). After this it's flat—almost. Breezing along on Chemin de la Pointe-Basse you'll be struck by how human landscape blends with nature. Pastel houses of blue, purple, and yellow float in a sea of green grass; brightly coloured clothes are strung out with arms and legs flapping in the wind. The lush, treeless hills ("buttes" in French), undulate on the horizon.

2.7 km (1.7 mi.)   Turn right on Chemin du Quai where there's a grocery store—Fabien Arseneau & Fils—and an Esso station.

The large grey building on your right was once a herring smokehouse. This used to be a flourishing industry on the islands. Peek inside and you'll see that the pointed roof is crisscrossed with a latticework of wooden beams. Rods packed with herring were hung there. The roof was left open to let the smoke escape, but the strong smell of smoked fish still permeates the building. You can still taste smoked herring in La Grave (Havre-Aubert). A dollar will buy you a delectable bagful of the stuff.

Just beyond the smokehouse, on the right, is a white building owned by Robert Noël de Tilly—master boat-builder and Mr. Hospitality. Peek inside the shop. You may see Robert—recogniz-

able by his swarthy beard, overalls, and cheerful, beaming face—
hunched under the keel of a wooden fishing boat. If he's not too
busy he'll gladly explain the process of building boats out of
fibreglass—right down to showing you the sheets of fibreglass
and the sticky, smelly stuff that glues the fibreglass onto the boat
frame.

In mid-July, the port of Pointe-Basse hosts the Festival des
Fruits de Mer (Seafood Festival). During lobster season (May 10
to July 10) you can buy fresh lobsters from fishermen unloading
their morning catch.

3.0 km (1.9 mi.)   Return to the intersection of Chemin des
Quai and Chemin de la Pointe-Basse, and turn right onto Chemin
de la Pointe-Basse.

Stop at the blue house (number 379), the yellow house (number
86), and the green house (number 95). They all show characteristics
of traditional Acadian architecture—distinctive triangular gables,
wooden shingles, guillotine windows, and intricate corbel designs
in each roof corner. Some say the bright colours are for the
tourists, so they can find their way back to the right bed and
breakfast. Indeed, some houses are used by the locals as landmarks. A friend of mine, Claude Richard, lives beside a large
CO-OP supermarket. For years he directed people to the blue
house beside the CO-OP. Ever since he repainted his place a shocking banana yellow—visible for miles— people joke that the
CO-OP is located beside the yellow house!

4.3 km (2.6 mi.)   Continue along Chemin de la Pointe-Basse
which turns into Chemin des Échoueries. Just after the dirt road,
stop on your right in the parking area facing the lighthouse.

What a perfect spot for picnic benches. This is one of the best
places on the islands to have a picnic, so if you didn't grab a bite
at Au Vieux Couvent stop here, and while you feast you can
admire two of the most famous sights on the Magdalen Islands—
the volcanic Buttes Pelées and Cap Alright. After lunch, follow
the path to the little red-and-white automated lighthouse, standing forever on guard on the Cap Alright promontory. The inter-
mittent beam of light this tiny beacon tosses out to sea has its
own distinctive pattern of flashes, which ships use to determine
their bearings. Past the lighthouse, the narrowing, wedge-shaped
point of Cap Alright overlooks a guano-laden islet packed with

Double-crested Cormorants and Black Guillemots. Out to sea, Île d'Entrée—the only inhabited and unconnected island in the chain—looms strikingly on the horizon. The 15-m (50-ft.) cliffs of this promontory are constantly eroding and quite unstable. Don't walk too close to the edge! There used to be a tall stack—naturally formed by erosion—at the tip of Cap Alright, which collapsed during a violent storm in 1968.

For a bird's-eye view of the entire archipelago climb to the summit of Butte Ronde, the mountain that's towering above you. From that vantage point, the lace-like string of islands seems to stretch endlessly to the north and south beneath you. For a full description of the route up Butte Ronde read Climbing Route 3 - Butte Ronde beginning on page 91.

If you're feeling adventuresome, you can also have a subterranean view of caverns, arches, and tunnels. Just before the lighthouse, close to the cliff, where the path dips into a ravine, you'll find a rope tied to a stake in the ground. You can climb down it to the beach at Anse à Firmin. The relentless attack of the sea on this promontory has carved out fascinating sculpted forms that you'll see as you get near the base of the cliffs. If you're going to climb down the rope it's best to have someone watching you.

5.3 km (3.3 mi.)   Stay on the dirt road until you reach Chemin des Montants. Turn right onto Chemin des Montants.

For the next kilometre, you'll either be huffing and puffing as you push your bicycle up the stony road over the summit of Buttes Pelées, or you'll be huffing and puffing from the seat of your bicycle. No matter how you do it, you'll be huffing and puffing up the steep road to the top! And it's worth it—for the unparalleled view and the downhill run right into the sea at Dune-du-Sud. Before you head down, there's a hike out to the craggy volcanic precipice of Buttes Pelées for some dizzying views. For directions see Climbing Route 5 - Buttes Pelées on page 105.

7.1 km (4.4 mi.)   At the fork in the road there is a Stop sign. Turn right onto Chemin de la Dune du Sud.

As you coast downhill to Dune-du-Sud, you'll glide by a peculiar object on your left lying on a well-manicured lawn. It's a brown barrel with a set of sails on it, and the inscription Winter Magdalen Mail. The story goes something like this: in 1910 the

only way that Magdalen Islanders could communicate with the mainland was by telegraph cable. That January the cable snapped, leaving them cut off from the rest of the country. To let people know of their predicament, the islanders outfitted a molasses barrel (or ponchon) with rudder and sails. On February 2 they launched it from Havre-Aubert carrying the Royal Mail and a letter to the minister of the navy informing him of the broken cable. In a few days, the vessel landed on the coast of Cape Breton. The contents were given the authorities and help was dispatched to the Magdalen Islands. You could say that the islanders got themselves out of a barrel of trouble with the ponchon!

8.0 km (5.0 mi.)   Stop opposite the Casse-croûte du Vieux Quai (the snack bar) in the picnic grounds and park at Dune-du-Sud.

The Dune du Sud beach is known locally as the "family beach," since it's mainly families who frequent the wind-protected bluffs. If you want to go where the action is—teenagers, volley-ball, and that sort of stuff—then you're looking for the Pedalo, just past the bridge connecting Havre aux Maisons with Cap aux Meules. What you'll find at Dune du Sud is some of the most fascinating formations carved into the craggy banks of these red headlands. Going right on the beach, you'll discover tunnels, grottoes, and all sorts of nooks and crannies formed by the sea. There's a narrow tunnel with just enough room for a thin person to walk in on one side and squeeze through to the other. I'll leave it to you to find it.

10.4 km (6.5 mi.)   Return to Chemin de la Dune du Sud and turn left. Follow the road until you reach the intersection of Highway 199. A sign on your left reads Cap-aux-Meules (8 km) and Grosse-Île (32 km). Turn left onto 199 West.

11.2 km (7.0 mi.)   On 199 West, you'll see a sign to turn left at La Méduse (glassblower). Turn left on the dirt road Chemin de la Carrière and follow the signs for La Méduse—Glassblower.

François Turbide—one of sixteen children—is a master glass-blower or gaffer. Like a magician, he twirls, spins, and gyrates a gob of orange molten glass, coaxing crude shapes into recogniz-able form. Vases, bowls, fruits, and crystal balls dancing with light are the end products of his wizardry. They adorn shelves throughout his studio. In 1979 François shaped his first bubble of

glass and was mesmerized by the molten mass. Years of studying in France, many exhibitions in Quebec, and in 1985 his own workshop—La Méduse—next to his home at Havre-aux-Maisons. If you arrive at his studio at the right time—usually midmorning—you can observe a piece being created. You'll see François jab a hollow cane into the "glory hole" and remove a fiery orange ball of liquid glass. The glory hole contains a mixture of sand, soda, and lime in exact proportions, at a temperature of about 1,200°C (2,300°F). Precise movements, contortions, and gyrations interspersed with quick bursts of breath into the cane will amaze you as a familiar shape emerges at its tip. Afterwards, you can wander around the saunalike studio and look at pieces for sale, as well as his private collection. Don't be surprised to hear the sheep bleating nearby. Half of the building is a barn with goats, chickens, and a family of cats strolling in and out.

11.4 km (7.1 mi.)   From La Méduse follow the dirt road back to Highway 199. Turn right onto 199 East.

You probably won't have to pedal even once on this long downhill stretch to the Galerie d'Art Point-Sud. But watch for the gallery's sign, or you may whistle right by it.

14.5 km (9.0 mi.)   Turn left at the sign for Galerie d'Art Point-Sud.

A visit to the Magdalen Islands without seeing the Galerie d'Art Point-Sud is like going to Paris and not visiting the Louvre—well, sort of. Rémi Bergeot and Micheline Couture, the curators/owners of the gallery, vacationed in the Magdalen Islands for years before succumbing completely to their spell. In 1987 they bought the "last house on Dune-du-Sud" and in 1988 officially opened the only art gallery in the Magdalen Islands. In their home-town of Montréal they are highly regarded in the fields of visual and textile art. They still teach there and often give solo exhibitions. They've both brought a great deal of energy and dedication to the islands, and they're committed to exhibiting multidisciplinary, contemporary art. Local artists like Carole Piédalue and Jean Luc Turbide, as well as artists from across Quebec, exhibit here every summer. If you can, try to make it to a vernissage (an opening). The unveiling of an artist's work creates a wonderful air of excitement and curiosity in the place. If you fall in love with one of the works but can't get it on your bicycle ... don't worry. Rémi will see it gets delivered to you.

17.0 km (10.5 mi.)   From the Galerie d'Art Point-Sud turn back onto 199 West and then turn right on Chemin du Cap-Rouge.

19.5 km (12.0 mi.)   At the yellow left-turn sign make a right onto Chemin des Cyr. (The sign is faded and difficult to read.) Chemin des Cyr will veer to the left and become a dirt road.

20.8 km (12.9 mi.)   Stop just past the grey house (number 170) on your right.

From the house, it's just a five-minute hike to the summit of Butte chez Mounette, an absolute must on your list of places to go. From this panoramic perch, the views of the Lagune du Havre aux Maisons, La Pointe, Île Rouge, Île aux Cochons, and the Dune du Nord are truly superb. For a full description of the route and sites from Butte chez Mounette read Climbing Route 6 - Butte chez Mounette on pages 109-113.

21.1 km (13.0 mi.)   Turn left off the dirt road onto a paved road Chemin de la Petite-Baie.

22.1 km. (13.7 mi.)   Turn right onto Chemin du Cap-Rouge.

22.8 km (14.1 mi.)   Turn left onto 199 East.

23.0 km (14.3 mi.)   Au Vieux Couvent Hotel, on the right, is the end of the line!

Cap à Gaspard

Route Length:
This hike is only .65 km (.4 mi.) long.

Approximate Time Required:
The climb to the summit and back takes just over fifteen minutes. Sitting on the terrace of Au Vieux Couvent sipping a glass of wine will undoubtedly take longer.

Terrain:
There's no clearly marked path to the top of Cap à Gaspard. From the starting point on the beach, just set your sights on the summit and make your way through the tall grass until you reach the 30.5-m (100-ft.) peak.

Difficulty:
This very easy, short climb can be done by anyone.

Precautions:
The route follows cliffs with sheer drops into the sea. Stay at least 6 m (20 ft.) from the edge, which can crumble beneath you. You'll wind your way through tall grass that may reach your waist. It is often very windy here, with frequent strong gusts at the top.

What to Wear/Bring:
Because of the tall, often prickly grass, I recommend long pants. Other than that, anything goes.

When to Go:
Any time of the day, but my preference is between 6:30 and 7:00 p.m. During this half-hour period, I often sit on the peak and watch the approach of the ferry—the *Lucy Maud Montgomery*—as it arrives from Prince Edward Island to dock at Cap-aux-Meules.

Points of Interest:
From Cap à Gaspard there are fabulous views of the island of Cap aux Meules.

Directions to Route Starting Point:

From the Tourist Bureau, turn right on Chemin Principal. Follow signs for 199 East, which will take you across a green bridge into Havre-aux-Maisons. On your right, just past the Irving station, you'll see a three-storey concrete building and a sign—Au Vieux Couvent Hotel. The route starts on the right-hand side of the hotel, next to the outdoor terrace. It's about 5 km (3 mi.) or a five-minute drive.

Route Description

I'm not sure whether Cap à Gaspard was named after Chez Gaspard—the bar in the basement of the Au Vieux Couvent Hotel—or vice versa. But before heading out, sit on the terrace facing the sea, and order a Moules Alfredo with a glass of white wine. If you're lucky, Reginald Poirier, one of the owners, might happen by. He'll answer the question—and tell you a lot more!

Breathtaking vistas of Île d'Entrée from Cap à Gaspard.

He'll undoubtedly tell you that the Au Vieux Couvent was built as a convent in 1917 by nuns of the Order of Notre-Dame des Flots, and that it's still the highest cut-stone building on the Magdalen Islands. He may also tell you that the Catholic church in front of the hotel burned down in 1973. The four owners of this historical building—Evangeline, Francine, Henri-Paul, and Reginald—have been gradually converting it. The dining room— La Moulière—was once a chapel. Ten classrooms have become guest rooms, and the Mother Superior's quarters have become

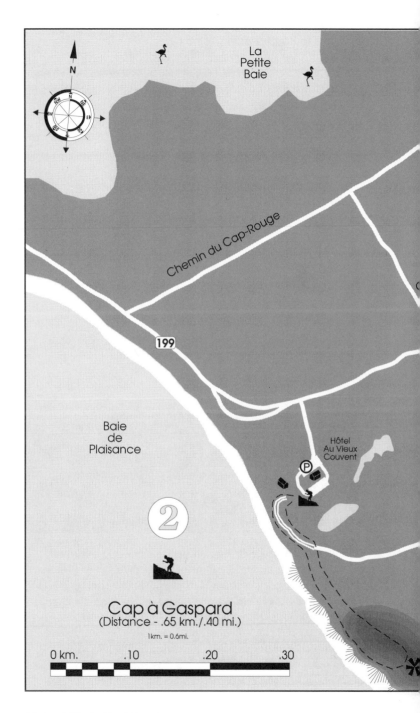

La
Petite
Baie

Chemin du Cap-Rouge

199

Baie
de
Plaisance

Hôtel
Au Vieux
Couvent

②

Cap à Gaspard
(Distance - .65 km./.40 mi.)

1km. = 0.6mi.

0 km.   .10   .20   .30

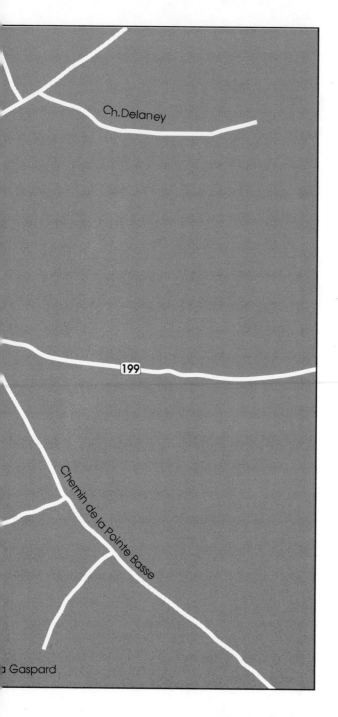

Ch.Delaney

199

Chemin de la Pointe Basse

Gaspard

the terrace and bar where you're sitting. Check out my favourite room—number twelve, affectionately known as the honeymoon suite—where three sets of weathered French windows face the open sea for a spectacular and romantic view.

After finishing your Moules Alfredo, white wine, and decadently rich French desert, you may have to muster all your willpower to climb to the summit of Cap à Gaspard—which you've been looking at for the past hour. I know, I've been there.

From the terrace, walk down the dirt road to the beach, passing a two-storey house on your right. On the beach, follow the double-track road until it meets up with a grassy area. At this grassy junction, veer right and make your way through the tall grass to the summit of Cap à Gaspard—a short five-minute climb.

Breathtaking vistas of Île d'Entrée, Havre Aubert, and Cap aux Meules unfold from the heights of Cap à Gaspard. Twice daily— at 7:00 a.m. and 7:00 p.m. you can watch as the glistening white ferryboat—the *Lucy Maud Montgomery*—cuts through the deep blue waters of the Gulf of St. Lawrence. To your left, is one of the few quarries still in operation on the Magdalen Islands. Rocks dug there are used to make breakwaters.

Brightly painted houses scattered over the hillside are traditional Acadian design. They're two stories high, rectangular, and have distinctive triangular gables, wooden shingles, and guillotine-type windows. But it's the colours that you'll never forget, especially when the sun illuminates their shocking purple, electric blue, banana yellow, and emerald green hues. Islanders compete annually for the Architectural Merit Award, so much thought goes into choosing a colour or a corbel design for a roof corner. You might say that each Madelinot's house reflects the personality of its owner.

When you feel the urge for an espresso or café au lait on the terrace of Au Vieux Couvent, retrace your steps and follow the coffee aroma coming from the hotel.

Butte Ronde

Route Length:
The distance to the summit and back is 1.2 km (.75 mi.).

Approximate Time Required:
It takes about twenty minutes to reach the cross atop Butte Ronde and another fifteen to get back down. You'll probably spend another half-hour looking around.

Terrain:
The first part of the climb is pretty flat and follows a well-defined path around the backside of the mountain to a barbed wire fence. From here on, the path's a little less clear, and it begins to rise more steeply towards the summit at 100 m (330 ft.).

Difficulty:
The first two-thirds of the way up can be done by almost anyone. The last section is a steep angle on a grassy slope, and it's a bit of a grind. Just pace yourself and you'll soon be at the summit.

Precautions:
Be careful when you're climbing beside the barbed wire fence. It's sometimes electrified with a very low current to discourage cows from climbing to the top. It wont' hurt you, but it'll get your attention. The grassy slope to the summit is very steep, and sometimes slippery, particularly on the way down. Mosquitoes aren't too bad, except on the occasional windless day. But put on mosquito repellent anyway. The summit has strong gusts, so stay back from steep edges and keep an eye on kids. If you're thinking of climbing up or down the rope, be warned that the small forest you'll pass through is swarming with the biggest, hungriest mosquitoes I've ever seen!

What to Wear/Bring:
Mosquito repellent—you'll be glad you listened to me! A light jacket's a good idea. When it's windy, it can be a little cool at the top. Hiking boots are a must for this hike. It's too slippery for bare feet, sandals, or running shoes. If you're going to climb the rope to the top, wear long pants, a long-sleeved shirt, and a jacket with a hood. The mosquitoes in this tiny forest area are ferocious!

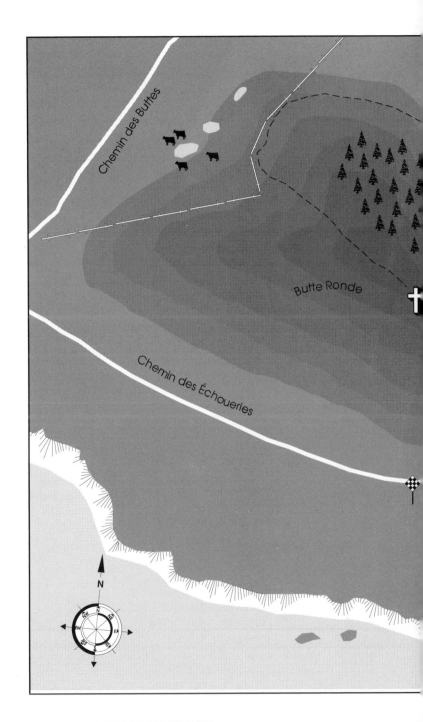

Chemin des Buttes

Butte Ronde

Chemin des Échoueries

N

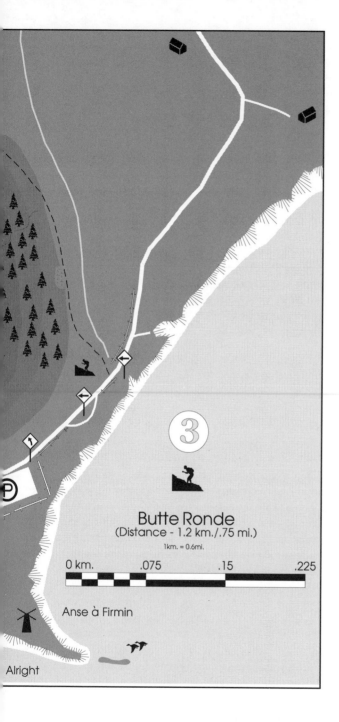

Butte Ronde
(Distance - 1.2 km./.75 mi.)

1km. = 0.6mi.

0 km.	.075	.15	.225

Anse à Firmin

Alright

When to Go:

Any time of the day is great, but I find just before sunrise the most beautiful. The cliffs of Buttes Pelées and Cap Alright catch the sun's rays and begin to glow in deep shades of red and orange that are reflected in the surrounding ocean. What a sight!

Points of Interest:

Views of Buttes Pelées, Cap Alright, Île d'Entrée and whole archipelago.

Directions to Route Starting Point:

From the Tourist Bureau, turn right on Chemin Principal. Follow signs for 199 East, which take you across a green bridge into Havre-aux-Maisons. A few hundred metres after passing the Au Vieux Couvent Hotel, turn right onto Chemin de la Pointe-Basse. Stay on Chemin de la Pointe-Basse (which becomes Chemin Échoueries) until it becomes a dirt road, about 50 m (160 ft.) along the dirt road, you will see a parking area with picnic tables on your right. From there, walk along the dirt road, passing two left-turn arrow signs. Just before the third left-turn arrow, you'll see a path to the summit on the left-hand side of the road. The path starts just in front of a fence. It's about 8 km (5 mi.)—a ten-minute car ride from the Tourist Bureau.

Route Description:

I thought I knew everything about climbing Butte Ronde. I was saved from possible embarrassment by my friend, Gil Thériault, who said that no guidebook to the Magdalen Islands would be complete if it didn't mention the short cut to the summit of Butte Ronde, via a rope—a route only the locals knew, and which he had taken frequently as a child. I searched in vain, scouring the mountain, but to no avail—I needed help. So one evening Gil, his dog, and a few friends showed me and my son Sean the well-hidden short cut to the top of Butte Ronde, which I'll describe as you follow my descriptive ascent to the peak.

When you arrive at the starting point, it's easy to see the well-trodden path to the summit. The path first dips into a gulley, then rises to road level before continuing along the south side of a small creek.

In a few minutes you'll pass a marshy area on the left that is often filled with the pungent aroma of mint. Wild mint is

abundant on the Magdalen Islands, growing in marshy areas or beside small creeks and ponds. If you've never seen mint plants, they're easily recognizable by their purple stem and pointed dark-green leaves. As a final test, smell the leaves, which give off a minty odour. The leaves make mint tea—great for digestion and for tranquil sleeping.

In early July, the route is often choked with wildflowers, bursting in a rainbow of colours. Fields of white daisies and purple irises are strewn throughout the green mountainside.

The short cut to the summit—by rope— is just past this marshy area, on your left. It's hard to find, but look carefully and you'll see a dark opening in the forest about 10 m (33 ft.) above the path. A path leads through the trees to a rope that's anchored at the summit. This short cut takes you to the top in about ten minutes. It's fun, but don't try it unless you're dressed from head to toe and have mosquito repellent on. Otherwise you'll be eaten alive—I mean it!

Those who don't want to be a mosquito's meal can just continue along the path. The trail veers upwards to the left until you reach a barbed wire fence. Walk beside the fence, but don't touch it. Occasionally there's a low voltage electric current running through it to stop cows from climbing Butte Ronde. Not that it'll damage you, but who needs the aggravation.

After climbing beside the fence for about 50 m (164 ft.), you'll

A small red-and-white lighthouse stands guard on Cap Alright.

be more or less parallel with some small ponds in the valley to your right. At this point, make a 90° turn and climb right to the top of Butte Ronde. The going's a little tougher here, but you'll soon see the cross on the summit. The 8.2-m (27-ft.) cross was built in 1981. It's lit up at night, making it a conspicuous landmark.

When you reach the top, take a deep breath and lie back in the grass for a well-deserved rest. The view can wait. To the north, the jagged edges of the volcanic Buttes Pelées seem to plunge vertically into the sea. (Many of the buttes on the island, including Butte Ronde, are volcanic—formed from the interactions of limestone, basalt, gypsum, and clay.) To the south, below you, is the tiny spit of land—Cap Alright—and the little red-and-white lighthouse that stands forever on guard. Havre aux Maisons was for many years named Île Alright, after this picturesque little cape. Until 1968 the cape had a naturally occurring pillarlike structure at the end. It collapsed in a violent storm.

Between May 10 and July 10, fishermen set their traps off the tip of Cap Alright. Hundreds of coloured buoys bob up and down in the sea swells. The colours identify each fisherman's trap. Occasionally, I've seen seals bobbing up and down too in Anse à Firmin.

Beyond Cap Alright, the sparsely populated Île d'Entrée sits serenely on the horizon. More than two hundred anglophones live quietly there. With binoculars you can see the guano-laden cliffs, home to thousands of sea birds that nest on precarious perches. Big Hill, at 174 m (571 ft.), is the highest point on the Magdalen Islands and is the third "hill" to the right of the cliffs.

On a very clear day, you can see Havre-Aubert at the southern end of the archipelago. The string of islands has a hook shape—at its tip, the dunes of Sandy Hook (Dune du Bout du Banc).

Follow the same route down, or, if you can't resist the urge to play Tarzan, grab the rope attached to the cross and scramble down to where it meets the trail. And say hello to the mosquitoes for me!

Cap Alright to Dune-du-Sud

Route Length:
The route is 7 km (4.3 mi.) long.

Approximate Time Required:
About four hours.

Terrain:
The hike starts on the narrow shoreline beneath the cliffs of
Buttes Pelées, where the terrain varies from sandy beaches to
stone beaches with rocky outcroppings. From the coastline, you'll
climb a 31-m (100-ft.) grassy slope to the plateau atop Dune du
Sud. From here, you have two routes to Chemin de la Dune du
Sud. You can continue along the plateau, or go down to the beach
at Dune du Sud. If you choose the beach route, you have to scam-
per down the red sandstone cliffs about 24 m (80 ft.). And you'll
get wet as you walk through an arch in a cliff where the sea
swells often reach your waist or higher. Whether you take the
beach route or the cliff route, they both end up at Chemin de la
Dune du Sud. The rest of the hike is along Chemin de la Dune du
Sud and Chemin des Montants—a steep gravel road that traverses
Buttes Pelées.

Difficulty:
Slippery boulders, rocky outcroppings, and steep slopes make this
four-hour hike more demanding than many in this book. If you
decide to call it quits at Dune du Sud—about the halfway mark—
you can call a taxi from the snack bar there and get a ride back to
your car. Knowing that it takes about two hours to reach the picnic area at Dune du Sud, I often arrange for someone to meet me
there. In any case, I've taken quite a few people on this hike—
including two women in their late fifties who had no problems at
all!

Precautions:
The trail hugs the thin strand of land between the sea on your
right and the cliffs of Buttes Pelées on your left. I've never experienced rock slides here, but you should be cautious. Definitely
don't try to climb these cliffs! The beach alternates between sand
and stones, and the stones are often quite slippery with algae.

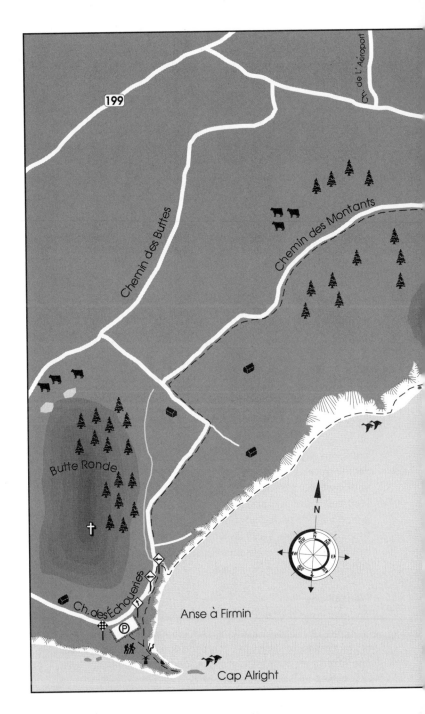

Ch.Boudreau

Ch.Chevarie

Ch.de la Dune du Sud

Dune-du-Sud

Cap Adèle

Buttes Pelées

*Bird-watching near
Dune du Sud.*

④

Cap Alright - Dune-du-Sud
(Distance - 7 km./4.3 mi.)

1km. = 0.6mi.

| 0 km. | .30 | .60 | .90 |

The currents are very strong, so if you swim, stay close to shore. The cliffs at Dune du Sud are unstable. Stay away from the edge.

What to Wear/Bring:

Hiking boots. If you wear sandals, running shoes, or try to go barefoot you'll have a lot of trouble negotiating the rocky outcroppings and slippery stones along the way. Bring a knapsack, for the treasures you'll find on the seashore, and binoculars to view the Black Guillemots and Double-crested Cormorants that nest on the cliffs. Carry drinking water, because there are no facilities until you reach Dune du Sud. A good walking stick will definitely come in handy.

When to Go:

This hike should be done only at low tide on calm, sunny days. If you call the Tourist Bureau (at 986-2245) they'll give you a daily schedule for low tide. Don't even think about this route on rainy days, or when the seas are rough!

Points of Interest:

The jagged rock formations carved into Buttes Pelées are especially striking when seen from below. The solitude, the muffled sound of surf crashing on the beach, and the sea gulls soaring high above the cliffs make this one of my favourite hikes.

Directions to Route Starting Point:

From the Tourist Bureau turn right on Chemin Principal. Follow signs for 199 East, across a green bridge into Havre-aux-Maisons. A few hundred metres past the Au Vieux Couvent Hotel, turn right onto Chemin de la Pointe-Basse. Stay on this road (which will become Chemin des Échoueries) until it becomes a dirt road. There's a parking area with picnic tables on your right about 50 m (164 ft.) along the dirt road. From the Tourist Bureau to here is about 8 km (5 mi.)—a ten-minute car ride.

Route Description:

Every time I turn the corner of Chemin des Échoueries, just past the lighthouse at Cap Alright, I'm struck by the grandeur of the Pelées cliffs—a bastion against the might of the sea. For years, the peaks beckoned me like a siren, but I thought it was impossible to walk the rocky shoreline. One day I couldn't resist the

temptation any longer, so my friend Claude Richard and I explored the uncharted territory around each craggy bend. Now I hike this exhilarating route every summer.

From the parking area, follow the path to the red-and-white automated lighthouse. Did you know that the red-and-white markings of lighthouses are called "daymarks"? They make the lighthouse as visible as possible in stormy weather. The set patterns of periodic flashes help ships know their location, because each lighthouse has its own pattern of light signals.

Continue past the lighthouse to Cap Alright—the tiny parcel of land jutting into the sea. The island of Havre aux Maisons was previously named Île Alright, perhaps after this promontory. Just off the tip of Cap Alright, colonies of Double-crested Cormorants and Black Guillemots queue up single file along the ledges of the islet.

Facing northwards from Cap Alright you can trace the shoreline route you're about to take. It may look impossible to walk beneath these massive cliffs, but trust me—it can be done, and it's worth the effort.

Heading back to the parking area, the path dips into a small ravine. At the edge of it, there's a rope tied to a stake. You can scramble down here to the rocky beach. At the bottom are fantastic views of sea caverns chiselled into the cliffs. Now and then I've caught glimpses of grey seals bobbing up and down in the sea—or were those buoys—left behind by fisherman to help identify the location of their lobster traps? If you climb down, make sure the rope and stake are secure—and have another person at the top.

When you reach the parking area, continue to the right along the dirt road (Chemin des Échoueries) passing three yellow left-turn signs. At the last sign on your right, follow the path down a ravine and over a drainage pipe to the beach. The small creek you've just passed over is one of the few on the island. Each island has it's own supply of ground water, which is very limited. If fresh water is pumped out faster than it's replenished by rain and snow seeping into the ground, saltwater seeps into the freshwater reserves and can endanger the islands' water supply. So plenty of rain is good for the Magdalens—although you don't want it today.

Turn left when you reach the sea. A sandy beach—with some small rocks—extends about .5 km (.31 mi.). If you walk close to

the cliffs, you'll see bright orange veins of gypsum running through the red sandstone. As you run your hands over the brittle sandstone, it'll crumble. That's how fragile it is. A thin layer of iron oxide gives the cliffs their distinctive reddish colour. Try not to get any red sandstone on your clothes—it's almost impossible to wash out.

Starfish, sand dollars, moon shells, razorshells, cockle shells, and intricate pieces of driftwood are some of the treasures cast ashore. The longshore current also strews the coastline with orange gloves (used by fishermen), pieces of yellow rope, cow bones, coloured foam buoys and mangled lobster cages. And who knows what else the sea may cast up? So keep your eyes peeled.

As you round the first bend, an immense rock with the profile of a baboon looms menacingly overhead. It seems to stare over the beach as though protecting its territory. You might try offering it a banana! Baboon Bend, at the .5-km (.31-mi.) point, is the first of four bends along the route.

Continue along a sandy beach covered with all sorts of slippery, slimy delicacies from the briny deep. Dulse, Wrack, Finger Kelp, Sugar Kelp, and Irish Moss blanket the foreshore. Did you know that wrack is rich in vitamins and minerals? It's used in ice cream, chewing gum, cosmetic creams, and water softeners. Carrying a good field guide will help you identify sea vegetation.

The sandy beach gradually gets rockier as you approach Seaweed Bend—the second bend in the route, about 1 km (.62 mi.) along. As you round Seaweed Bend, the larger rocks give way to a stone beach.

Approaching the third bend, you'll see in the distance a black spire rising squarely from the sea. As you get nearer, the beach becomes rockier. Just past the ravine, you'll begin to make out the shape of cormorants perched atop the ominous black stack. This bizarre work of nature is about 6 m (20 ft.) high and 3 m (10 ft.) in diameter.

At the third bend—Cormorant Bend—you'll be dwarfed beneath the highest cliffs of Buttes Pelées—vaulting over 110 m (360 ft.). The razor-sharp ridges and pinnacles are speckled with Black Guillemots and breeding sea birds. These cliff dwellers feed on the crustaceans that inhabit the intertidal zone.

Gypsum Bend—the last bend—is not far now, and from here onwards the large boulders and sheer cliffs melt into soft red headlands and green valleys. When you reach Gypsum Bend look behind

and above for dramatic views of the needlelike volcanic peaks.

The last stretch of sandy beach past Gypsum Bend ends abruptly at an unpassable promontory. Turn left at this point and you'll see a yellow rope at the base of the hill. Use the rope to scramble up the slope, making sure that you veer towards the plateau on the right. At the top, follow the plateau to the tip of the promontory for a view of the cormorants and some small islands.

Take a long look around, pick some strawberries, or lie in the field of daisies. Eventually, you can decide which way to go from here.

You can continue along the plateau overlooking the beaches and cliff formations of Dune du Sud. The more adventuresome option is to scramble down the sandstone cliff, just past the promontory, to the sandy beach below. If you take this route, be prepared to get wet. You'll pass under an arch in the headland where the waves swell to your waist. The beaches of Dune du Sud are very popular with families because the bluffs provide protection from the wind. The craggy ridges have tunnels, caves, and all sorts of nooks and crannies carved out of them. Can you find the one with the tunnel?

The last segment of the route—if you're energetic enough—follows Chemin de la Dune du Sud, left onto Chemin des Montants and then back to the start. This could take another two hours. If you opt for a taxi instead, who's to know.

5

Les Buttes Pelées

Route Length:
This circular route, along the highest cliffs on the Magdalen Islands, covers 1.12 km (.7 mi.).

Approximate Time Required:
The entire hike can be completed in about thirty minutes, and from the start it only takes ten minutes to reach the lofty summit of Buttes Pelées. This is one of the best places on the Magdalen Islands for a romantic wine and cheese picnic lunch on the heavenly heights.

Picnic atop the Buttes Pelées.

Terrain:
There's no clearly marked path, but most of the trail is alongside a wire fence, up the grassy slope to the summit at—110 m (360 ft.). The last stretch to the top is on a steep but manageable incline, about 100 m (328 ft.) long. A walking stick would come in handy for this climb.

Difficulty:
Over the past fifteen years, I've taken hundreds of people on this route—from eight-year-olds to seventy-five-year-olds. In other words, you don't have to be an olympic athlete to enjoy this route.

Precaution:
The Buttes Pelées have the highest and steepest cliffs on the islands (except for Île d'Entrée and Butte du Vent). Stay at least 9 m (30 ft.) from the edge. The summit can be very windy. Occasionally, the barbed wire fence along this route is electrified. Its low current won't harm you—it's meant to keep cows away from the cliffs. At the start of the hike you have to climb this fence. I use a fallen fence post to push the wire down, then step over it. Cows often graze here, and they could care less about you.

What to Wear/Bring:
Because it's often windy on the summit, I recommend a light jacket. Wear hiking boots. (The grassy slopes are sometimes slippery.) Binoculars will help you see the Black Guillemots and cormorants on Cap Adèle and to scan the open horizon.

When to Go:
Just about any time of day, but wait for clear weather so you'll have the incredible views. I suggest planning your hike around a gourmet picnic of fresh lobster and wine at some idylllic spot. But don't let me influence you!

Points of Interest:
From this 110-m (360-ft.) pinnacle, the croissant-shaped archipelago spreads out beneath you. And all around it is the sea. It's from here that you can really appreciate the delicate beauty of these islands.

Directions to Route Starting Point:
From the Tourist Bureau, turn right on Chemin Principal. Follow signs for 199 East, across a green bridge into Havre-aux-Maisons. A few hundred metres past Au Vieux Couvent Hotel, turn right onto Chemin de la Pointe-Basse. Stay on this road, which becomes Chemin des Échoueries and then a dirt road. Follow the dirt road past the lighthouse, until you reach the first intersection. Turn right onto another dirt road (Chemin des Montants) and follow it to the summit. When you begin to descend—about 200 m (656 ft.) down—there's a sharp turn to the left. You should be able to see the airport, dunes, and horseracing track on your left. Stop here. Cross the barbed wire fence—to your right—and start climbing. It's about 11 km (7 mi.) from the Tourist Bureau to here—a fifteen-minute drive.

Route Description:
Moo-oo! Moo-oo! Moo-oo! That's probably the first sound you'll hear as you start your climb. As you gaze over the emerald green slopes, reminiscent of Ireland, the silhouettes of cows against an impossible blue sky dot the landscape. Meandering nonchalantly on the steep hills, these sure-footed animals will watch your progression to the summit of Butte Pelées with seeming indifference—or perhaps a quizzical

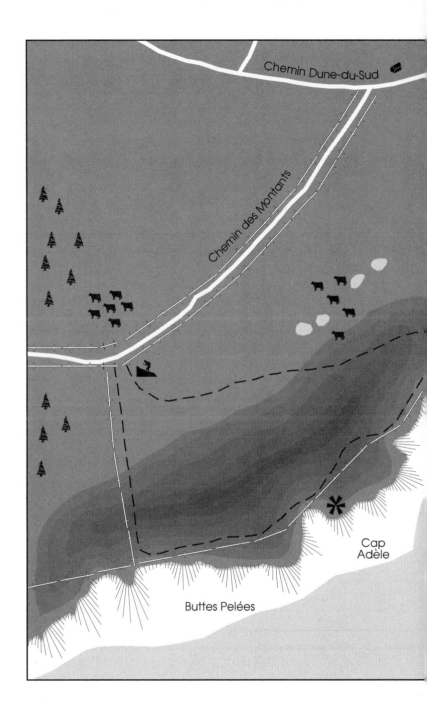

Chemin Dune-du-Sud

Chemin des Montants

Cap
Adèle

Buttes Pelées

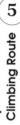

Hiking along the boulder-strewn coastline near Cap Adèle.

From the 110-m (360-ft) pinnacle of Buttes Pelées, the entire croissant-shaped archipelago stretches into the distance.

Les Buttes Pelées
(Distance - 1.12 km./.7 mi.)

1km. = 0.6mi.

stare. Dont' mind the cows, but keep an eye out for the "cow patties."

To cross the fence, find a hardy piece of wood and push down the barbed wire, then cautiously step over it. Year after year, I've used the same wooden post, always putting it back in the same place. If you're lucky, it's waiting there for you. Please leave it where you found it.

After crossing the fence, continue walking parallel with it towards the cliffs (as shown on the map). I bet you're wondering what all those small green mounds are. They're cow patties that, over the years have frozen and thawed to produce little bumps of earth.

In springtime, these fields become a yellow sea of dandelions—the cows eat the "sea." Dandelions increase the quantity of milk given by a cow and improve its quality. In parts of the world dandelion roots are used as a coffee substitute, and in the Maritimes and Newfoundland the leaves are used in salads and the yellow flowery heads as an ingredient for wine.

It'll take about five minutes to get to the edge of the cliffs. Turn left and follow the fence up the steep rise to the summit of Buttes Pelées, keeping well back from the edge. From the craggy, volcanic peak, the view is awesome. You can see both ends of the archipelago—Grande Entrée to your left and Havre Aubert and Île d'Entrée to your right. Here, you don't contemplate sea and sky—they just overwhelm you.

Follow the fence down into the valley, where you can have your wine and cheese picnic. If you brought your binoculars, you can spy on the whitewashed promontory to your left where cormorants and guillemots stand single file like an army facing the sea.

The return route passes a row of small ponds before coming back to the barbed wire fence, which leads you to where you started to climb. Near these ponds, several years ago, a group I was leading was confronted by what looked like a large menacing black bull with huge horns. Much to our relief, it was a cow—at least that's what we were later told.

Butte chez Mounette

Route Length:
From the base of the hill to the summit and back is .4 km (.25 mi.). It's probably easier to measure the distance for this climb by the number of steps you take. For me, it was three hundred.

Approximate Time Required:
It takes you only five minutes to reach the top of Butte chez Mounette, but it'll take you a lot longer than that to leave. Trust me!

Terrain:
Standing on the road, looking to the top of Butte chez Mounette, you should be able to see a path leading to the top. If you can't, don't worry about it—just pick your way as you go. The path winds up a grassy slope to the 61-m (200-ft.) summit. The incline is pretty gradual.

Difficulty:
A great hike for everybody. It's so easy that my two sons, Sean and Ryan—at ages five and two—enjoy racing one another to the top.

Precautions:
Sometimes the grass on the way up can be slippery, especially in the early morning before the dew evaporates. Mosquitoes can be bothersome at the summit or when there's no wind.

What to Wear/Bring:
Mosquito repellent. And it's best to put it on before you start climbing, because they won't give you a chance once you reach the top. It can be cool and windy, so bring a light jacket. And your binoculars—the birds on Île Rouge and Île aux Cochons are waiting.

When to Go:
My favourite time to climb Butte chez Mounette, which I've done countless times with my family, is just before sunset. When you reach the top, take a front row seat for nature's majestic show—a fiery red ball slowly slipping behind Dune du Nord seems to

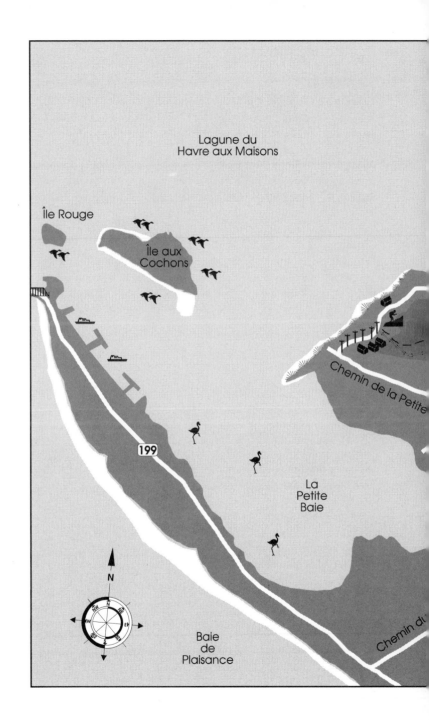

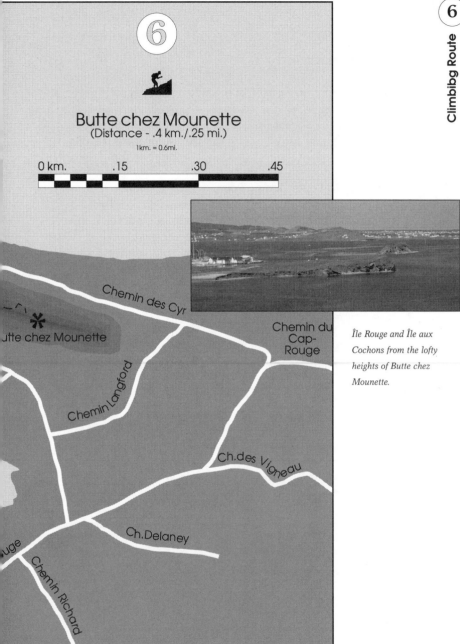

⑥

Butte chez Mounette
(Distance - .4 km./.25 mi.)

1km. = 0.6mi.

0 km.   .15   .30   .45

Île Rouge and Île aux Cochons from the lofty heights of Butte chez Mounette.

sizzle into the sea. The sky and clouds are often set aglow after the sun has disappeared.

Points of Interest:

It's impossible to pick a favourite hike on the Magdalens, but this one's right up there because of the indescribable sunsets over Dune du Nord. Watching and listening to hundreds of birds soaring over Île aux Cochons and Île Rouge—not to mention the breathtaking views in all directions—makes this climb a special one.

Directions to Route Starting Point:

From the Tourist Bureau, turn right onto Chemin Principal. Follow signs for 199 East, across a green bridge into Havre-aux-Maisons. At the intersection of Highway 199 and Chemin du Cap-Rouge turn left (there's an Irving station at this corner). Turn left again at Chemin de la Petite-Baie and follow it until it becomes a dirt road. Make a right on the dirt road (it's called Chemin des Cyr) and pass six hydro poles and a grey chalet (number 208). Park your car on the side of the dirt road. The climb to the top of Butte chez Mounette starts to the right of the fence that is just past the chalet, where you'll see a path to the top. It's about 7 km (4.3 mi.) from the Tourist Bureau to here—ten minutes by car.

Route Description:

On some old maps of Havre aux Maisons, Butte chez Mounette was called Mont Alice, and I used to call it that. For years I drew blank expressions when I said I was going to hike up Mont Alice. One day I pointed out the summit to my friend Reginald Poirier from the steps of Au Vieux Couvent Hotel. He quickly corrected my geographical faux pas, saying it was Butte chez Mounette, and that it was probably named after Cap à Mounette—the cape across the road from the hill (butte). In the Magdalen Islands you'll often find that place names on a map are called something else by the locals.

From the road, look towards the summit of Butte chez Mounette. Whether or not you see the path, the directions are easy—set your sights on the top and climb until you reach the plateau.

In just a few minutes, you'll be there.

To the north, you'll see the runway of the Magdalen Islands

Airport. It opened in 1960 as House Harbour Airport. Before the airport was built, planes landed on the beaches of Havre Aubert, Fatima, and Havre aux Basques. Imagine stepping out of a plane right onto the beach! The new terminal, built in 1982, handles about 45,000 passengers a year. More than 80,000 kg (176,000 lb.) of lobster leave here annually for all over the world.

Facing west, you can see the Dune du Nord stretching for over 20 km (12.4 mi.) to the tiny enclave of Île aux Loups. The dunes enclose the Lagune du Havre aux Maisons. Blue Mussel farming in the lagoon has become an important industry on the islands. The lagoon also attracts the grey seal, often seen on deserted beaches.

Looking south you'll see a narrow wisp of land called La Pointe and attached to it the marina of Havre aux Maisons. A bit further to the right, the green steel bridge connecting Havre aux Maisons with Cap aux Meules crosses the channel of Havre aux Maisons. For years a rickety, twisty, covered wooden bridge joined the two communities.

Directly opposite the bridge is Île Rouge and just in front of it Île aux Cochons. These two tiny islands are teeming with birds jostling for space. There are Herring Gulls, Great Black-backed Gulls, Common Terns, Great Blue Herons, Double-crested Cormorants, Caspian Terns, and Semipalmated Plovers—amongst others. With binoculars you can see the soldierlike line formation that the Double-crested Cormorants maintain along the guano-saturated cliffs of Île Rouge. At sunset, the entire lagoon, including La Petite Baie, becomes a feeding ground for the Great Blue Heron, which can be seen standing motionless in the water awaiting its next meal.

The large warehouselike building to the right of the bridge is the Delaney Lobster Plant. In season it's overflowing with tanks of lobsters to be shipped around the world. The Magdalen Islands export over 1.5 million kg (3.3 million lb.) each year. Some islanders say the lobsters caught on the rocky sea bottom off the Magdalen Islands taste better than those caught on muddy sea beds because they don't ingest mud. You can taste the difference, they'll tell you.

Watch a Magdalen Island sunset from Butte chez Mounette before heading down. The islands are famous for them. I guarantee that the image of a huge, red sun slowly dipping into the sea and setting the sky on fire will be etched into your memory forever.

Icarus Flying Services

Rocher aux Oiseaux (Bird Rock Island)

"Nothing but blue skies..." you hum to yourself when you get to the tiny Magdalen Islands Airport. Inside the terminal, you begin to have second thoughts about this junket. Icarus Airlines? What kind of a name's that to inspire customer confidence? Didn't he follow a bad flight plan? The drone of an engine. From the corner of your eye you see a red-and-blue twin engine Britten Norman Islander on the tarmac inching towards the terminal building—and right on time too.

The pilot climbs out of the sleek cockpit—wearing shorts, sandals, a T-shirt, and tinted glasses. A sudden wave of panic strikes as you step out onto the runway and are greeted by Craig Quinn, aviator. He ushers you into the spacious ten-seater plane, and within minutes his reassuring smile and soft-spoken manner have soothed your nerves—somewhat.

You're lined up, staring down the runway—dials spinning, switches clicking, gauges and needles twirling. An incomprehensible chatter from the tower is the takeoff signal. The steady drone of the engines erupts into a deafening roar as the small plane lurches forward under full throttle. In seconds you're airborne and banking right over the Lagune du Havre aux Maisons —on your way to Rocher aux Oiseaux, a microscopic speck of rock in the middle of the great Gulf of St. Lawrence. Much to your relief Craig tells you he has over twenty-one years of flying experience. He sure knows the Magdalens, too. He's forty-three, was born on Île d'Entrée, and now lives in L'Étang-du-Nord.

Squinting out from side to side you'll soar over the golden beaches of Dune du Nord, hemmed in by a bottomless blue sea and the calm waters of the Lagune du Havre aux Maisons. What looks like a Caribbean island is Pointe-aux-Loups.

In about ten minutes you're passing high above the cliffs of Cap du Dauphin, bearing down on the lighthouse at Cap Noddy on the western edge of Île Brion.

A steep banking turn to the right past the lighthouse, and Craig brings the nose down a bit so that you're flying level with the red cliffs of Cap Clair, Pointe Dandy, and Cap à Bill. Tunnels, caves, grottoes, coves, and beaches streak by at 259 km (160 mph). It's hard to believe Craig when he tells you he's landed planes on the beaches of Île Brion.

As the last jagged rocks of the most easterly point of Île Brion fade out of view, the plane gently climbs higher and higher—in search of Rocher aux Oiseaux (Bird Rock Island). From this altitude, the vast empty expanse of the Gulf of St. Lawrence sweeps endlessly in all directions. Seconds and then minutes pass with no land in sight. You begin to get nervous again. Then you see it, off in the distance through the haze: a mammoth, green-capped dome surrounded by a shimmering sea. The plane starts descending as you near Rocher aux Oiseaux. Soon, recognizable shapes can be seen atop the cliffs. A scattering of houses, a lighthouse, and a radio tower cap the vaulting precipices that appear to be floating on the edge of oblivion. As you get even closer, a sight

Tens of thousands of birds crowd the rocky pinnacles of Rocher aux Oiseaux.

beyond imagination— tens of thousands of birds crowding the face of the rocky pinnacles. Murres, razorbills, puffins, and gannets angrily take flight and swarm the sky. Once, twice, and then perhaps a third time, Craig will circle this rock lost in the middle of nowhere, before levelling off and heading back to the safety of the archipelago.

Craig's airplane excursions to Rocher aux Oiseaux usually last about an hour and a half. He also flies over the southern portion of the islands—Cap aux Meules, Havre Aubert, Île d'Entrée and L'Étang-du-Nord. The highlights of that trip are the Elephant Rock at Le Gros Cap, the dunes of Dune du Bout de Banc (Sandy Hook), the cliffs of Île d'Entrée, shipwrecks along Dune de l'Ouest, the caves of La Belle Anse, and seals in Lagune du Havre aux Maisons. This trip lasts about an hour. Along the way Craig sometimes does a few acrobatic manoeuvres—a nose-dive for an up-close glimpse of the seals in Lagune du Havre aux Maisons, or maybe a fly-by over the ridiculously short and precarious landing strip on Île d'Entrée. You might ask him why he chose his company's name.

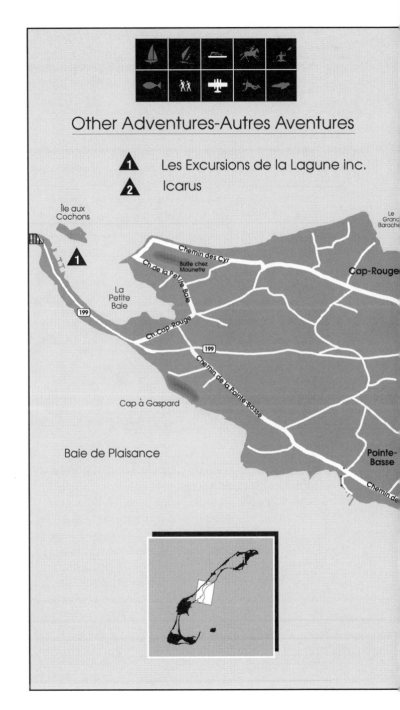

Other Adventures-Autres Aventures

1 Les Excursions de la Lagune inc.

2 Icarus

Île aux Cochons

Le Grand Barachois

Chemin des Cyr

Butte chez Mounette

Ch. de la Petite Baie

Cap-Rouge

La Petite Baie

199

Ch. Cap-Rouge

199

Chemin de la Pointe-Basse

Cap à Gaspard

Baie de Plaisance

Pointe-Basse

Chemin de

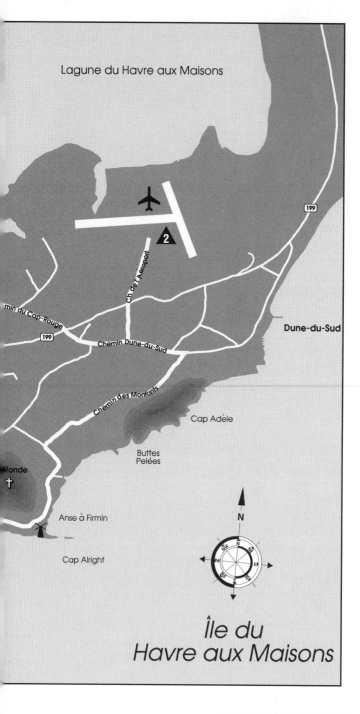

Lagune du Havre aux Maisons

199

2

Ch. de l'Aéroport

min du Cap-Rouge

199

Chemin Dune-du-Sud

Dune-du-Sud

Chemin des Montants

Cap Adèle

Buttes
Pelées

Ronde
†

Anse à Firmin

Cap Alright

N

Île du
Havre aux Maisons

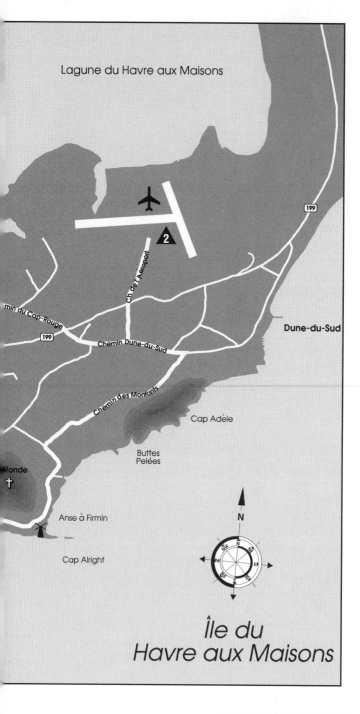

How to get to Icarus Flying Services:

Icarus Flying Services is located at the airport on Havre-aux-Maisons. From the Tourist Bureau, turn right on Chemin Principal. Follow signs for 199 East, across a green bridge into Havre-aux-Maisons. Continue along 199 East, following signs for the airport. At Chemin de l'Aéroport turn left until you reach the terminal building. Usually Craig will have arranged to meet you at the airport. If he's not there, try his hangar—turn left at the first dirt road along Chemin de l'Aéroport on your way back to Highway 199. It takes about fifteen minutes to reach the airport—9 km (5.5 mi.) from the Tourist Bureau.

For further information:

To inquire about prices or signing up on an excursion call (418)-986-6067.

Les Excursions de la Lagune Inc.

Glass-bottom boat
Exploration of Lagune du Havre aux Maisons:

The word lagoon conjures up images of mystery, shipwrecks, and lost treasures. A blue-and-white boat with a glass bottom—*Le Ponton II*—sails from La Pointe marina every day to reveal the secrets beneath the still blue waters of Lagune du Havre aux Maisons. Through the glass hull you can observe the teeming aquatic life in the lagoon. Demonstrations of lobster fishing, Blue Mussel harvesting, and the chance to sample freshly cooked lobster make for a unique sea adventure.

How to get there:

Les Excursions de la Lagune Inc. is located at the marina of La Pointe on Havre aux Maisons. From the Tourist Bureau, turn right on Chemin Principal and follow signs for 199 East, across a green bridge into Havre-aux-Maisons. Just past the bridge turn left after the Delaney Lobster building into the marina. It's about 4 km (2.5 mi.) from the Tourist Bureau—five minutes by car.

For Further information:

To inquire about prices, departure times, or to make a reservation call any of these numbers: (418) 969-4550, (418) 969-2088, (418) 969-2727.

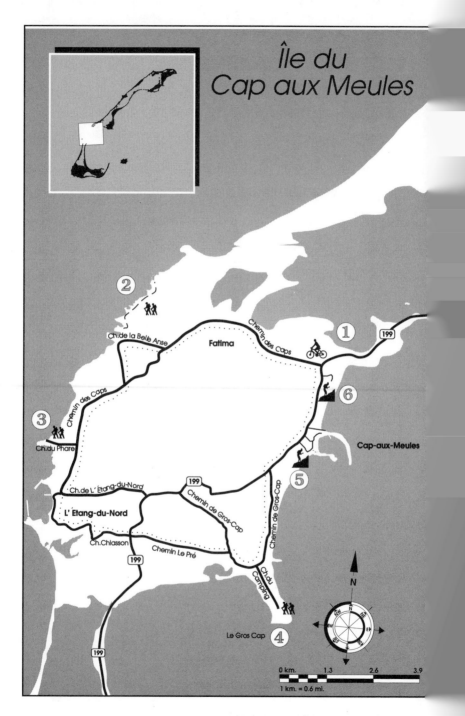

Île du
Cap aux Meules

Chemin des Caps

Ch.de la Belle Anse

Fatima

Chemin des Caps

199

Ch.du Phare

Ch.de L' Étang-du-Nord

L' Étang-du-Nord

199

Chemin de Gros-Cap

Chemin de Gros-Cap

Cap-aux-Meules

Ch.Chiasson

Chemin Le Pré

199

Ch.du Camping

Le Gros Cap

N

0 km.   1.3   2.6   3.9
1 km. = 0.6 mi.

ADVENTURES ON THE ISLAND OF CAP AUX MEULES

Cap aux Meules

Route Length:
This cycling route is 29.2 km (18.1 mi.) long.

Approximate Time Required:
A leisurely four hours will get you around the whole island of Cap aux Meules, with plenty of time left over to explore the scenic sites along the way—and there are quite a few.

Terrain:
Fortunately, this circular route skirts one of the highest mountains on the Magdalen Islands—Butte du Vent—without climbing an inch of it. Except for one fairly steep ascent near the end of the tour the cycling's pretty easy—I promise.

Road conditions:
Chemin des Caps, Chemin de la Belle-Anse, Chemin Boisville Ouest, Chemin Chiasson, Chemin Le Pré and Chemin de Gros-Cap are well-paved roads with very light traffic. The last segment of about 3 km (2 mi.) is on Chemin Principal (or Highway 199), which is the main thoroughfare through the city of Cap-aux-Meules. This road can often be congested with local and tourist traffic, and you should be cautious. Stay on the right-hand side of the road, or on the designated shoulder wherever possible.

What to Wear/Bring:
You'll be cycling through one of the more populated islands, so you'll find just about everything you need en route. But don't forget binoculars to observe the birds at Île aux Goélands and Cap du Phare. Wear what seems right for that day, but carry other clothes as the weather can change quickly. It could be from raingear to shorts and T-shirt or vice versa.

Precautions:
There's not much to worry about on this route. If you plan to stop and hike along La Belle Anse, Cap du Phare, Le Gros-Cap, or Buttes du Cap-aux-Meules remember the general warning about cliff edges. Stay well away from them. Take it as a given that cliffs in the Magdalens are unstable.

Difficulty:

This route—as with most cycling on Cap aux Meules—is easy, relaxing, and filled with interesting sights. It's a great outing for the whole family.

Facilities:

There are plenty of gas stations, restaurants, and grocery stores throughout the ride.

Points of Interest:

1) The shell shaped church at Fatima—Notre-Dame-du-Rosaire; 2) sea-sculpted islands, caves, and grottoes at La Belle Anse; 3) lighthouse at Cap du Phare; 4) fishing port at L'Étang-du-Nord; 5) shipwreck at Cap à Savage and birds on Île aux Goélands; 6) the elephant-shaped rock at Le Gros Cap; 7) seafood canning plant and restaurant at Pêcheries Gros-Cap; 8) view of port of Cap-aux-Meules from Butte du Cap-aux-Meules.

Directions to Route Starting Point:

From the Tourist Bureau, turn right on Chemin Principal following signs for 199 East. On your right you'll see the Hotel Château Madelinot, which is where the route begins. It's about 1.2 km (.75 mi.) from the Tourist Bureau—two minutes by car.

Route Description:

0.0 km (0.0 mi.)   From the Château Madelinot cross Highway 199 (Chemin Principal) onto the scenic road—Chemin des Caps—following signs for Fatima.

1.0 km (.62 mi.)   At the intersection and Stop sign veer to the right, continuing on Chemin des Caps.

2.1 km (1.3 mi.)   Just past the Baie du Cap Vert you'll begin to climb a small hill that's .6 km (.37 mi.) to the top.

3.5 km (2.17 mi.)   Chemin des Caps turns sharply to the left at Chemin de L'Hôpital and continues into the village of Fatima.

4.6 km (2.85 mi.)   Proceed along Chemin des Caps into Fatima and stop on your left at the white shell-shaped church—Notre-Dame-de-Rosaire.

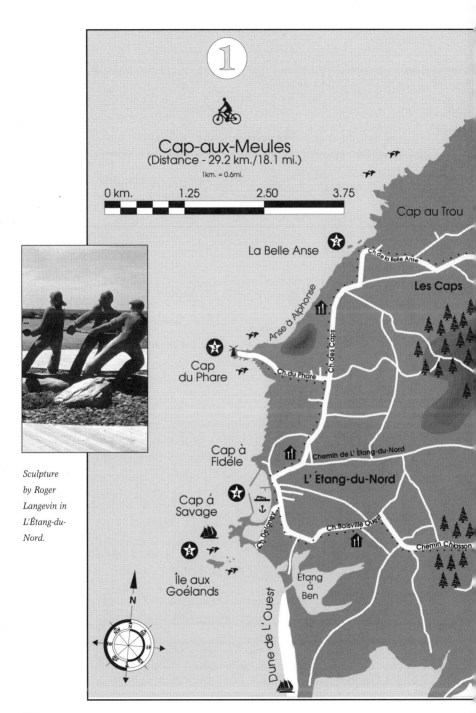

①

Cap-aux-Meules
(Distance - 29.2 km./18.1 mi.)
1km. = 0.6mi.

0 km.   1.25   2.50   3.75

Cap au Trou

La Belle Anse

Ch. de la Belle Anse

Les Caps

Anse à Alphonse

Ch. des Caps

Cap
du Phare

Ch. du Phare

Cap à
Fidéle

Chemin de L' Étang-du-Nord

L' Étang-du-Nord

Cap á
Savage

Ch. Delaney

Ch. Boisville Ouest

Chemin Chiasson

Île aux
Goélands

N

Etang
à
Ben

Dune de L'Ouest

*Sculpture
by Roger
Langevin in
L'Étang-du-
Nord.*

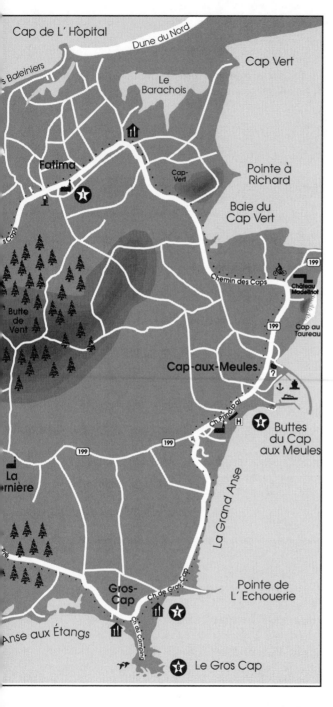

Stop and take a peek at this unique and beautiful church. From the outside, Notre-Dame-de-Rosaire's modern religious architecture resembles a seashell. Inside, you may feel as if you're on a boat instead of in a church. Some of the windows are shaped like portholes. Other symbols of the sea adorn the church.

7.2 km (4.46 mi.) After visiting the church, keep going on Chemin des Caps. Turn right onto Chemin de la Belle-Anse. Watch carefully for the turn-off. It's easy to miss since it's on a short downhill.

8.2 km (5.08 mi.) Arrive at La Belle Anse.
La Belle Anse is famous for two things—its fanciful sea-sculpted rock formations and spectacular sunsets. Waves pounding relentlessly on the delicate sandstone have carved grottoes, pillars, caverns, and sinkholes into the red headlands. But don't get too close to the edges—they are extremely dangerous! For a more detailed description of the area and sites at La Belle Anse read Hiking Route 2: La Belle Anse - Cap au Trou beginning on page 129 in Chapter 6.

8.7 km (5.4 mi.) From La Belle Anse turn right and continue to the intersection. Turn right onto Chemin des Caps.
You are now in Les Caps, one of three regions in the municipality of Fatima. The other two are Cap-Vert and Grand-Ruisseau. Les Caps is named after the high cliffs in the neighbourhood. If you look straight ahead before you turn right on Chemin des Caps, you'll see the second highest point on the Magdalen Islands—Butte du Vent. Radio Canada and the community station (CFIM) have antennas atop its 161-m (543-ft.) summit.

10.3 km (6.38 mi.) Turn right off Chemin des Caps onto Chemin du Phare. It's easy to miss this turn as it's on a downhill slope.

11.1 km (6.88 mi.) Arrive at Cap du Phare.
You can cycle up the red-dirt road to the lighthouse at Cap du Phare. From the tip of the cape there are indescribable views of the bird-filled Île aux Goélands, le Corps Mort (Dead Man's Island), and the Port of L'Étang-du-Nord. You can even see the rusting remains of a massive shipwreck off Cap à Savage. For a more detailed description of the area and sites at Cap du Phare

read Hiking Route 3: Cap du Phare on page 134 in Chapter 6.

11.9 km (7.37 mi.) Cycle back along Chemin du Phare and turn right on Chemin des Caps.

13.2 km (8.18 mi.) Arrive at the Stop sign and intersection with Chemin de L'Étang-du-Nord. Turn right onto Chemin de L'Étang-du-Nord and continue to the port.

13.6 km (8.43 mi.) Welcome to the quaint fishing port of L'Étang-du-Nord. Straight ahead you'll see a sculpture of seven fishermen pulling on a rope. Roger Langevin's *Les Pêcheurs* ("The Fishermen") was erected in 1990. Stroll along the recently built boardwalk and through the park. L'Étang-du-Nord was named after the small pond just south of this harbour. Every July, L'Étang-du-Nord hosts the Festival du Pêcheur—one of the largest outdoor festivals on the Magdalens. The Blessing of the Boats, a fishermen's mass, children's day, clowns, fireworks, and local music groups like Suroît draws people from far and wide for a day of joie de vivre.

Just to the left of the port, off Chemin Boisville Ouest, is a large wooden building known as La Côte. Don't miss the opportunity of going inside. There's a permanent interpretive exhibit on the history, heritage, and traditions of L'Étang-du-Nord, depicted in text and photographs.

14.3 km (8.86 mi.) Turn left on Chemin Boisville Ouest, then right on Chemin Delaney. Follow it to the beach.

Leave your bicycle on the beach and turn right—towards Île aux Goélands (Gull Island), a stone's throw off the coast. With binoculars you can see the many species of gulls that nest there. On a clear day, you might spot Le Corps Mort (Dead Man's Island), an immense, grey rock—as inhospitable as its name suggests—floating in the shimmering sea about 10 km (6 mi.) from the western tip of Havre Aubert. Le Corps Mort is barren and perpetually shrouded in fog. The *Berwindlea* (1935), the *Beater* (1957), and the *Laura* (1868) are amongst the many ships that have been wrecked on this menacing reef.

There are shipwrecks to be seen nearby. Walk to the end of the beach and climb the path to Cap à Savage, staying well back from the cliff edge.

The path leads to a massive rusting hulk just off the tip of the cape. It's the remains of a dry dock—one of two that were being towed from Montréal to Sydney, Nova Scotia, when a storm struck on December 22, 1988. They broke loose in the fierce seas—the other one coming to rest at Dune du Nord near Pointe-aux-Loups.

If you have binoculars, scour the Dune de l'Ouest, to the south. You may detect the skeletal remains of a Greek ship—the *Corfu Island*—that sank on December 20,1963, in a violent storm. Artifacts salvaged from the wreck are on display at the Musée de la Mer (Sea Museum), in La Grave (Havre-Aubert)—including its last S.O.S.

15.9 km (9.85 mi.)   Turn back onto Chemin Delaney and continue to Chemin Boisville Ouest. Turn right onto Chemin Boisville Ouest.

17.7 km (10.97 mi.)   Stay on Chemin Boisville Ouest until you reach Chemin Chiasson. Turn right onto Chemin Chiasson.

19.3 km (11.96 mi.)   Arrive at the intersection of Chemin Chiasson and Chemin Martinique (Highway 199). Cross Chemin Martinique and continue on Chemin Le Pré.

From the intersection of Chemin Chiasson and Chemin Martinique, if you look to your left, you'll see the white wooden church of Saint-Pierre La Vernière, which dominates the landscape. It was built in 1876 and is listed as an historical monument. A visit to the church is just a short detour about 2.5 km (1.55 mi.) to the left along Chemin Martinique (Highway 199 East).

Another worthwhile detour is about the same distance—2.5 km (1.55 mi.)—to the right along Chemin Martinique. It's the La Bouillée de Bois self-guided nature trail (next to Camping La Martinique). It's a forest with elfinwood and White and Black spruce and has interpretive signs. If you take either or both of these detours, remember to come back to the intersection to find your cycling route.

22.3 km (13.82 mi.)   From Chemin Le Pré turn right onto Chemin du Camping.

22.8 km (14.13 mi.)   Arrive at Parc Gros-Cap.

The Elephant, a massive rock that looks uncannily like said animal, stands just off the point of Le Gros Cap—as though it were wading there. See it now—in not too many years the power of the waves may have undermined the strength of the Elephant. Before going to see this landmark, you'll have to ask permission from the park attendants in the gatehouse. Campers pay to stay overnight in the park, but just say you're going to visit the Elephant. They'll understand. For a more detailed description of the area and sites at Le Gros Cap read Hiking Route 4: Le Gros Cap on page 139 in Chapter 6.

23.2 km (14.38 mi.)   Cycle back along Chemin du Camping and turn right onto Chemin de Gros-Cap.

25.0 km (14.88 mi.)   Continue along Chemin de Gros-Cap and stop on your right at the Pêcheries Gros-Cap Inc.

The Pêcheries Gros-Cap Inc. was founded in 1932 by twelve fishermen from the Magdalens as the Grindstone Fishermen's Association. In 1944 it became the Co-opérative du Gros-Cap and then took its present name. Stop here if you like eating seafood—especially lobster—or just to tour the facility.

Delicious snow crab, scallops, or lobster—freshly cooked, frozen, or canned—are sold here. Upstairs, at

the cafeteria-style restaurant—La Factrie—you can watch lobster being prepared for export (through a window), while savouring your own delectable crustacean fresh from the morning's catch!

The white wooden church Saint-Pierre in La Vernière.

26.3 km (16.30 mi.)   From the Pêcheries Gros-Cap, turn right onto Chemin de Gros Cap. Turn right again onto Chemin Principal (Highway 199 East).

27.0 km (16.74 mi.)   From Chemin Principal, turn right

onto Chemin du Quai. Stop beside the Excursions en Mer (sea tours) sign, just past the C.T.M.A. building. From here, you can climb to the summit of Butte du Cap-aux-Meules.

The observation point atop Butte du Cap-aux-Meules provides a sensational panorama of Cap-aux-Meules and the private marina—La Marina, Club Nautique. For a more detailed description of the area and sites from Butte du Cap-aux-Meules read Climbing Route 5: Butte du Cap-aux-Meules on page 143 in Chapter 6.

29.2 km (18.10 mi.)   Go back up Chemin du Quai and turn right on Chemin Principal (Highway 199 East). Climb the hill past the Tourist Bureau and stop at the Château Madelinot.

Congratulations, you've completed the bicycle tour of Cap aux Meules! You will likely have an appetite after the tour. For supper, I recommend Diane Vigneau's gastronomical restaurant—also in the Château Madelinot—overlooking the sea. Try her pot en pot and tarte au sucre with crème des Îles.

La Belle Anse to Cap au Trou

Route Length:
The round trip 1.65 km (1.02 mi.) long.

Approximate Time Required:
It's an easy, two-hour trek. But the irresistible sunset at La Belle Anse takes at least another thirty minutes.

Terrain:
There's not one hill to climb. In two spots you'll traverse a marshy area and you'll also go through a small forest. The cliffs in this region are about 12 m (40 ft.) high. There's no clearly defined path for this hike, but parts of the route are beside a double-track road that's shown on the map.

Difficulty:
This is a very relaxing hike that almost anyone can complete without difficulty.

Precautions:
As always, stay well away from the edge of cliffs. Near the end of the route there's a large sinkhole. It appears suddenly, and has some pretty steep ridges.

What to Wear/Bring:
Hiking boots are best—preferably waterproof—since there are wet marshy areas to cross.

When to Go:
Any time's great, but I recommend near sunset, so you can watch the sun slip into the sea.

Points of Interest:
La Belle Anse is famous for two things—the fascinating, sea-sculpted rock formations and awesome sunsets. You'll get to see both.

Directions to Route Starting Point:
From the Tourist Bureau, turn left on Chemin Principal following signs for 199 West. At the first set of lights—turn right and

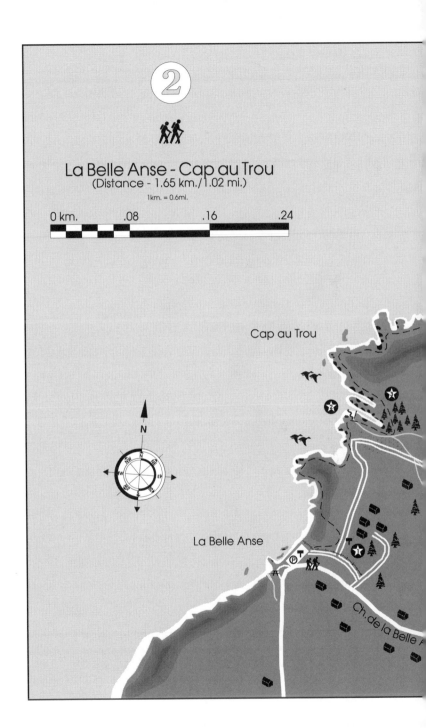

2

La Belle Anse - Cap au Trou
(Distance - 1.65 km./1.02 mi.)

1km. = 0.6mi.

0 km.   .08   .16   .24

Cap au Trou

N

La Belle Anse

Ch. de la Belle A

Gazing at the fascinating sea-sculpted rock formations at La Belle Anse.

continue on Chemin Pettipas past the horse racing track to the Esso station at Chemin des Caps. Turn left onto Chemin des Caps and continue to Chemin de la Belle-Anse. Turn right onto Chemin de la Belle-Anse and follow the road until the curve. Turn right, into the parking area. It's about 10 km (6 mi.) from the Tourist Bureau—ten minutes by car.

Seaside bluffs thrust upwards towards an aquamarine sky at La Belle Anse.

Route Description:

La Belle Anse is one of those rare places that have a mystical beauty which captivates the soul. The sea and wind have carved astonishing formations into the rocky red headlands. Grottoes, pillars, and caverns dot the promontory. The mysterious sinkholes resonate when the sea rushes into them.

La Belle Anse isn't a secret anymore—a slow but steady stream of sunset worshippers arrives to watch the fiery red ball sizzle into the sea.

From the parking area, walk over to the Explorivage exhibit. It depicts, through photographs, how erosion has transformed the cliffs over the years. It's a vivid reminder, too, of what I keep repeating—the instability of these cliffs.

There's no distinct path to follow on this hike, so I've identified five reference points, which are shown on the map. Watch out for them, and you'll keep your bearings. It's hard to get lost here anyway, because you're following the coastline both ways.

The reference points are:

1. Site # 4 Demonstration Site—La Forêt Rabougrie put up by the environmental group Attention Frag'Îles.

2. Stake and rope on the cliff (opposite the green and purple house). This is a marshy area.

3. Path through forest and around cave-filled headland.

4. A second marshy area with a river that flows to the sea.

5. Large sinkhole.

This hike takes you away from the crowds at La Belle Anse into a tranquil region where you can hear the birds chirping and smell the elfinwood trees.

The next step's up to you. Pass through the fence at one of many spaces between posts and follow the double-track road, my reference points, and your compass, and you'll do just fine.

Besides the caverns, arches, and islets, you'll see fields of purple irises, blueberries, and Swallowtail Butterflies. If you read the Demonstration Site panels (reference point 1) you'll get a good idea of what flora and fauna inhabit the region.

The cliffs and caves on this stretch of coastline are home not only to nesting seabirds such as guillemots and Double-crested Cormorants—but hordes of sparrows. Fox Sparrows, Song sparrows and White-throated Sparrows dwell in the underbrush and often dart in front of you as you approach.

Don't be surprised to spot a group of yellow kayaks weaving in and out of the bays. On calm days many of the grottoes and caves can be explored at sea level.

At reference point 4, just where the creek meets the ocean, there's a wonderful little tidal pool in a cavern. Clamber down to see it and to hear the hollow sound of the sea rushing in to fill the pool. It's a great place to swim if the sea is calm and you don't mind the water being a bit chilly.

The last reference point before you head back to La Belle Anse is an amazing 11-m (40-ft.) wide sinkhole with an equally impressive arch that opens up to the sea. You can walk its perimeter, but don't get too close to the edges.

On the way back to La Belle Anse enjoy the solitude, serenity, and beauty of the sun setting in the gulf.

③ Cap du Phare

Route Length:
This hike around the Cap du Phare peninsula is .75 km. (.45 mi.) long.

Approximate Time Required:
Forty-five minutes will get you around Cap du Phare and back to your starting point.

Terrain:
A portion of the route follows a double-track road alongside the northern cliffs of the cape. The rest meanders over brittle sandstone. Most of the walk is flat with some gently rolling contours. The cliffs are about 15 m (50 ft.) above the sea.

Difficulty:
This is another hike for the whole family. Remember to keep children well back from the cliff edge.

Precautions:
These cliffs are unstable—don't walk too close to the edge. There are dangerous areas, where sinkholes and caverns have formed in the sandstone. These are marked on the maps with black circles.

What to Wear/Bring:
Except for a sturdy pair of hiking boots wear whatever the weather suggests. Binoculars are almost mandatory in the Magdalens because of the endless vistas—and should you want to look into a bird's eye.

When to Go:
Any time!

Points of Interest:
Look for the automated lighthouse at the tip of the cape and the unusual ringlike formations etched into the brittle sandstone cliffs. The views of Île aux Goélands, Le Corps Mort, and the harbour of L'Étang-du-Nord. And don't forget the massive shipwreck off Cap à Savage.

Directions to Route Starting Point:

From the Tourist Bureau, turn left on Chemin Principal following signs for 199 West. After passing the white wooden church at La Vernière, you'll see a sign for L'Étang-du-Nord. Continue towards L'Étang-du-Nord. When you reach the sign for Fatima turn right, onto Chemin des Caps. Turn left at Chemin du Phare and follow the road to the end. It's about 10 km (6.2 mi.) from the Tourist Bureau—fifteen minutes by car.

The port at L'Étang-du-Nord.

Route Description:

Lighthouses have an almost irresistible allure. Is it the pull of land's end or the sense of security their beacons provide? Hiking along the cliffs of Cap du Phare (Lighthouse Cape) you'll pass the towering red-and-white landmark that rises above the cape.

From the end of Chemin du Phare, follow the red-dirt road north to the cliffs near Anse à Alphonse. The craggy ridge extends for many kilometres up the coast—to La Belle Anse and beyond.

As you pass the lighthouse—which is now fully automated— you'll enter an area where the red sandstone has formed layer upon layer of ringlike shelves, or steps. On these shelves, you'll find the oddest objects—a single claw from a lobster, a dried out crab, empty clam shells. How did they all get here? I'll give you a clue—think of birds.

The birds snatch crustaceans from the sea and drop them onto the cliffs to break their hard shells and expose the delectable meat inside.

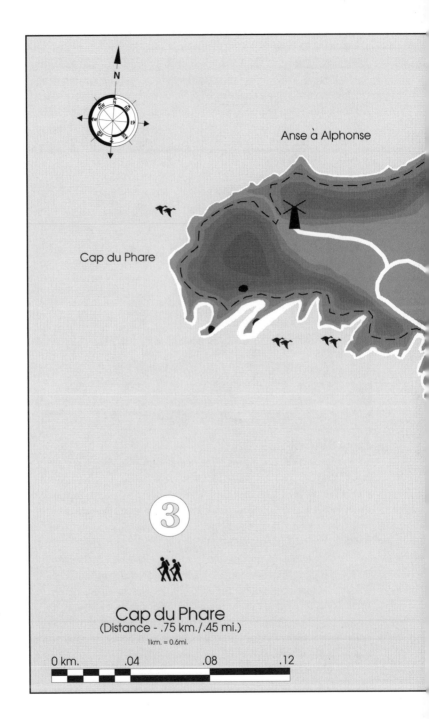

Anse à Alphonse

Cap du Phare

③

Cap du Phare
(Distance - .75 km./.45 mi.)

1km. = 0.6mi.

0 km.   .04   .08   .12

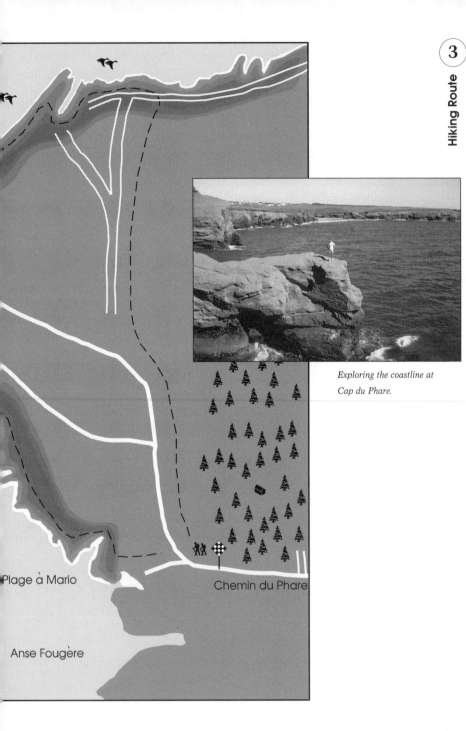

Exploring the coastline at
Cap du Phare.

Plage à Mario

Chemin du Phare

Anse Fougère

Looking southwestward from the tip of Cap du Phare you'll
see an immense grey island floating in the shimmering sea. Le
Corps Mort (Dead Man's Island) is just over 10 km (6 mi.) from
the western edge of Île du Havre Aubert.

Perpetually shrouded in fog, uninhabited, and without vegetation, this inhospitable rock got its name from its resemblance to
a human corpse. A constant menace to ships, Dead Man's Island
is the site of numerous tragedies. The *Berwindlea* (1935), the
Beater (1957), and the *Laura* (1868) are just a few of the many
vessels that have gone down here.

Hundreds of seals enjoy the remoteness of Le Corps Mort,
using the sunken ships as playgrounds and places to bask in the
sun.

A bit more to the south, and only a few kilometres from Cap
du Phare, is the port of L'Étang-du-Nord, named for the small
pond near the harbour. Directly behind the harbour is Cap à
Savage, site of another wreck—not a ship, this time, but a dry
dock. On December 22, 1988, two massive dry docks broke loose
in a storm while being towed from Montréal to Sydney, Nova
Scotia. One landed at Cap à Savage and the other at Dune du
Nord, near Pointe-aux-Loups. The other one has been dismantled
and used for scrap iron. May the rusting eyesore at Cap à Savage
soon meet with the same fortune!

To the left of Cap à Savage you'll see Île aux Goélands—or
Gull Island. Guess how it got its name.

Continue along the cliffs back to the start of this route. Watch
for the beautiful formations the sea has carved into the sandstone, and be on the lookout for sinkholes so you don't step into
one.

Le Gros Cap

Route Length:
This hike is only .85 km (.53 mi.) long.

Approximate Time Required:
It takes about forty-five minutes to complete the circuit.

Terrain:
You'll be walking on the crest of the 15-m (50-ft.) cliffs that border the Gros Cap peninsula. The terrain is level and follows an unmarked path beside a wooden fence enclosing the Gros Cap peninsula. Part of the route traverses a stunted forest area at the tip of Gros Cap.

Difficulty:
This is an easy, invigorating walk that's great for everyone.

Precautions:
The wooden fence encircling the peninsula is there for a very good reason—to discourage anyone from walking along the extremely unstable cliffs. Should you feel tempted to hop it for a closer look at the cliffs—please don't. After crossing the Stunted Forest you'll reach the tip of Le Gros Cap, where you'll see a deep sinkhole that's fenced off. Stay outside the fence—believe me, it's dangerous!

What to Wear/Bring:
The Gros Cap peninsula is very windy, so bring a windbreaker.

When to Go:
Any time's great, but I've found that at sunrise the cliffs radiate a red glow that's reflected in the calm early morning sea.

Points of Interest:
The Elephant, a massive rock shaped like its name, wades in the sea just off the point of Le Gros Cap. You have to see it—and soon! Such is the rate of erosion and topographic change in the Magdalens that before long the sea may have swallowed the Elephant.

Distance to Route Starting Point:
From the Tourist Bureau, turn left on Chemin Principal following

Plage á Aurelie

Anse aux Étangs

Chemin du Camping

④

Le Gros Cap
(Distance - .85 km./.53 mi.)

1km. = 0.6mi.

0 km.   .05   .10   .15

Plage des Sept Pierres

Baie de Plaisance

N

Cap Rouge

L'Éléphant

Le Gros Cap

The Elephant—a massive rock in the shape of a pachyderm— stands just off the point of Le Gros Cap.

signs for 199 West. Pass two traffic lights and the Place des Îles shopping centre. Turn left on Chemin du Gros-Cap and right on Chemin du Camping. Pass the signs for Parc du Gros Cap, and park to the right of the gates in the visitor parking area. From the Tourist Bureau to here is about 7 km (5 mi.)—ten mintues by car.

Route Description:

When I heard about the Elephant at Gros Cap, I thought the Magdalens were a strange place indeed. When I went there, and saw my mistake, I didn't change my mind about the islands' singularity. After all, a stone elephant standing in the sea, is a unique sight.

Before beginning the Gros Cap hike, tell the park attendants in the gatehouse that you want to visit the Elephant. Campers pay to stay here overnight, but people often pass through just to see the pachyderm. Ask out of courtesy.

From the gatehouse, turn left. Follow the dirt road past the picnic benches, then veer right towards the wooden fence by the cliffs. When you reach the fence, turn right. Walk beside the fence until you reach the Stunted Forest and the view of the Elephant. It was connected to the mainland by an arch, until erosion cut it off. Who knows when it will completely vanish beneath the waves?

Along the way you'll see other striking formations that the sea has chiselled out of the brittle red headlands—rocky outcroppings, islands, sinkholes, caverns, arches, tunnels, and indescribable fractures and fissures. And all over these fanciful escarpments—birds.

You may see scuba divers from Aventure Plongée exploring the caverns. One moment they're bobbing up and down in the sea, then they vanish. The caves have been given fanciful names by those who've been inside them—Dragon's Belly, Washing Machine, and the Cathedral.

Past the Elephant, the trail continues into the small forest. Turn away from the fence and backtrack until you reach a small opening in the trees. (Don't try to walk beside the fence as the trees from here onwards block the path.) It takes only a few minutes to emerge on the other side of the forest.

Return to the gatehouse by following the fence. The vast deserted beach on your left is the Plage de la Martinique. It and the Plage de l'Ouest form giant pincers enclosing the lagoon—Baie du Havre aux Basques.

Butte du Cap-aux-Meules

Route Length:
This is the shortest route in the book—.15 km (.10 mi.). I prefer to measure the climb in steps. It took me 183 steps to the summit and the same number back. Just a suggestion—not everyone likes to count their steps.

Approximate Time Required:
It's five minutes each way, but that's not the point of the climb. Allow yourself another forty-five minutes to watch the ferry arrive—or just to sit atop Butte du Cap-aux-Meules.

Terrain:
There's a clearly marked path to the peak, and there are even steps carved into the hillside near the top. The summit is 40 m (130 ft.) high, and the slope's enough to make you catch your breath.

Precautions:
At the top, stay back from the cliff edge. At the beginning of the climb, there are some loose stones.

Difficulty:
An easy climb for most people. Kids can do it in a flash.

What to Wear/Bring:
Hiking boots and a warm windbreaker. Binoculars—for the big picture.

When to Go:
Six-thirty in the evening's my choice becasue I find the hustle and bustle of the ferry's arrival at Cap-aux-Meules mesmerizing.

Points of Interest:
From the hilltop you can see the entire port of Cap-aux-Meules and the private marina La Marina, Club Nautique. Watching the ferry arrive at Cap-aux-Meules is a special treat.

Directions to Route Starting Point:
From the Tourist Bureau, turn left on Chemin Principal following

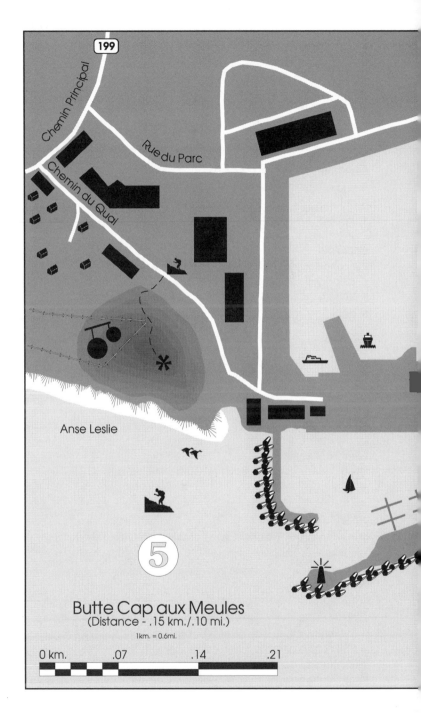

199

Chemin Principal

Rue du Parc

Chemin du Quai

Anse Leslie

⑤

Butte Cap aux Meules
(Distance - .15 km./.10 mi.)

1km. = 0.6mi.

0 km.   .07   .14   .21

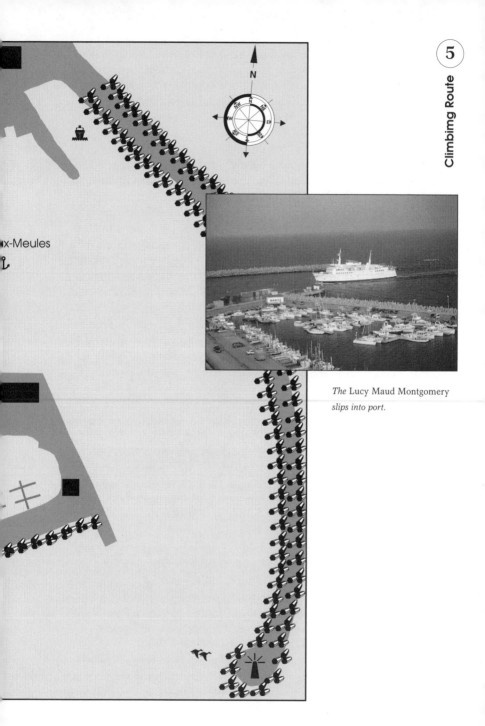

N

x-Meules

The Lucy Maud Montgomery
slips into port.

signs for 199 West. Turn left again onto Chemin du Quai. Stop on your right just past the white building with blue windows—the C.T.M.A. building. The path starts beside the sign for Excursions en Mer. It's about 1 km (.6 mi.) from the Tourist Bureau to here—about two minutes by car.

Route Description:

If you want to get a sense of everyday life and tradition in the Magdalen Islands, you should experience the daily ritual of the ferry's arrival at Cap-aux-Meules. It's still a major event for islanders who remember when the ferry was the sole link to the outside world—bringing supplies and news from far off places.

There's no better place to watch the ritual unfold than from the top of Butte du Cap aux Meules. By the way, "meules" means grindstone. The Island of Cap aux Meules was named after this hill, which is composed of the sandstone used to make grindstones.

To the right of the Excursions en Mer sign you'll see the path that winds to the top. Along your way, you'll skirt around a fence that surrounds the Irving fuel reservoirs. Monstrous tanks feed oil via underground pipes to the diesel powered Centrale Thermique electricity plant, which should be visible further to the south. An oil tanker docks at Cap-aux-Meules regularly to fill these reservoirs. Five minutes to the top guarantees the best seat in the house.

Beneath you, on Chemin de Quai, is the huge Madelipêche fish plant that processes ocean perch, cod, and flounder. The blue and grey trawlers in the harbour catch mostly ocean perch. The plant employs about four hundred people and processes more than 15,000 metric tons (16,530 tons) of ocean perch a year. You're welcome to take a look inside.

Across from the Madelipêche Plant is the head office of the C.T.M.A., or Coopérative de Transport Maritime et Aérien. Founded on May 28, 1944, the C.T.M.A. operates the cargo ship *Voyageur* and the *Lucy Maud Montgomery* (the ferry). The *Voyageur* carries freight between Montréal and the Magdalen Islands. It leaves Montréal every Friday and arrives in the Magdalens on Sunday afternoon—a distance of 1,050 km (650 mi.).

The *Lucy Maud Montgomery* ferry operates between Souris, Prince Edward Island, and Cap-aux-Meules. It can carry up to four hundred people and ninety cars. The 100-km (62-mi.) voyage

takes five hours, and there are two trips every day except Tuesday. The *Lucy Maud Montgomery* became the Magdalens' ferry in 1975, but for years before that it sailed between Prince Edward Island and Wood Islands, New Brunswick. You can set your watch by its schedule. It arrives at 7:00 a.m. and 7:00 p.m. every day—on the dot.

Directly beneath Butte du Cap-aux-Meules is the Canadian Coastguard station. It's distinctive red-and-white ships are moored opposite the building. Adjacent to the Coastguard boats is the terminal for the *S.P. Bonaventure* ferry to Île d'Entrée.

The croissant-shaped breakwater that protects Cap-aux-Meules harbour was built in 1970 using about 363,000 metric tons (400,000 tons) of stone and more than 11,000 dolosse. A strange name, indeed—and the concrete blocks that make up the break-water certainly have an unusual shape. Dolos (the singular spelling of dolosse) is a South African word meaning the knuckle-bone of a sheep. I presume they're shaped something like that, and I believe that the blocks were developed in South Africa.

Off in the distance you should be able to spot the *Lucy Maud Montgomery*—still just a white speck approaching Île d'Entrée. From there it's another half-hour before the ferry steams into harbour. Already you'll see people milling around the wharf. More cars keep arriving. It's almost 7:00 p.m., and even from up here you can sense the excitement.

The *Lucy Maud Montgomery* glides gracefully past the breakwa-ter and blows its horn.

The docking is a series of gentle nudges, coordinated by the captain over a walkie-talkie. At his command, a bow line is thrown out. The bow door begins to move upwards, and then the watertight steel doors open lower, like a drawbridge, until they crash against the steel dock.

Within moments a parade of tractor trailers, buses, motorcy-cles, trucks, cars, bicycles, and people spill onto the wharf.

The whole ritual has a similar excitement to waiting for a train. I never tire of it, especially watching the ship open up and disgorge its passengers. Children are fascinated by the whole spectacle.

With clockwork precision the ferry is unloaded, then reloaded for the trip back to Prince Edward Island.

I like to wave goodbye to the *Lucy Maud Montgomery* as she sails silently out of port—the setting sun's rays glistening on her white bow. Try it.

Cap au Taureau

Route Length:
This is the second shortest route in the book—a roundtrip distance of .2 km (.12 mi.).

Approximate Time Required:
Five minutes to the top of Cap au Taureau and an even easier five minutes back down.

Terrain:
The climb follows a double-track dirt road to the 55-m (180-ft.) peak.

Precautions:
You should keep a safe distance. Stay at least 10 m (30 ft.) back from the unstable cliff edge which is extremely fragile. Believe me, there's good reason for the repetition!

Difficulty:
This is the easiest climb in the Magdalen Islands.

What to Wear/Bring:
Whatever you want. But don't forget the binoculars—especially on this route. You'll be people-watching this time, not bird-watching.

When to Go:
About 6:30 p.m. By the time you get to the top of the cape, the *Lucy Maud Montgomery* will be approaching Cap-aux-Meules on her voyage from Prince Edward Island.

Points of Interest:
From the heights of Cap au Taureau you have a majestic view of the village of Cap-aux-Meules and the ferry's arrival.

Directions to Route Starting Point:
From the Tourist Bureau, turn right on Chemin Principal following signs for 199 East. Go up the hill, passing the Hotel Bellevue on the right. Not far past the hotel there's a grey building with a red roof and the sign—Garage-J. Harvie. Turn right on the first dirt road past the garage. Follow it until you reach another double-

track road that veers to the right. Stop here. From the Tourist Bureau to here is about 2 km (1.2 mi.)—two minutes by car.

Route Description:

Like its counterpart across the harbour—Butte du Cap-aux-Meules —Cap au Taureau is a favorite destination for some islanders. They can't get enough of watching the ferry arrive—and I can see why. To get there, just head up the double-track road. In five minutes you'll be sitting on top of the world.

The town of Cap-aux-Meules—the largest community and the hub of activity for the archipelago—sprawls in all directions. Picture-perfect houses cling to the sides of Butte du Vent—the second highest point on the Magdalen Islands, towering 161 m (543 ft.) above the sea. The fish processing plant by the harbour is swarming with activity as the catch of the day is unloaded from the trawlers. A giant crane shuffles boats in the drydock—its huge straps gently cradling the keel. The Hotel Bellevue, Pizza Patio, Auberge de la Jetée, Pharmaprix, and a string of boutiques, garages, and stores line either side of Rue Principal—Highway 199—the lifeline of the archipelago.

The dazzling white ferry blows its horn as it arrives. Bang on 7:00 p.m. as usual and ready to let out a parade of vehicles and pedestrians. See the spectacle once, and you'll begin to understand why the island tradition of watching the boat dock has

Cap au Taureau is a favourite destination for many islanders who end the day watching the arrival of the ferryboat— Lucy Maud Montgomery.

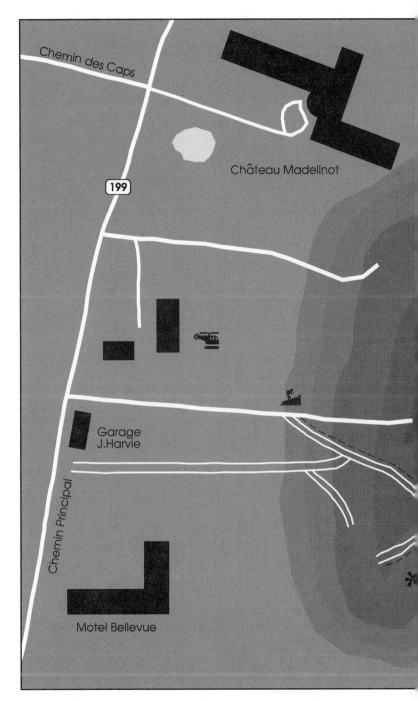

Chemin des Caps

199

Château Madelinot

Chemin Principal

Garage
J.Harvie

Motel Bellevue

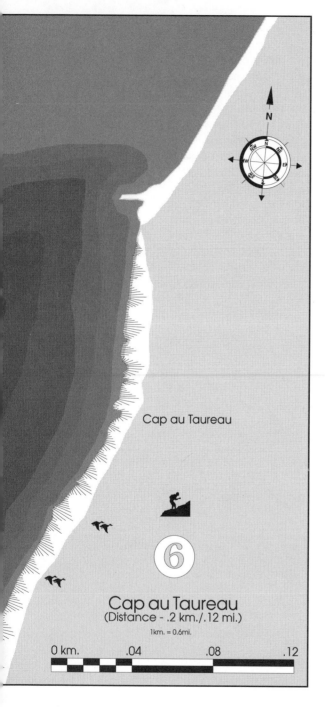

N

Cap au Taureau

6

Cap au Taureau
(Distance - .2 km./.12 mi.)

1km. = 0.6mi.

0 km.   .04   .08   .12

endured year after year. I must have seen it a hundred times with my children, and I bet you'll want to go back for more.

As soon as the bow doors open and the watertight doors are lowered, every vehicle that emerges from the ferry is on centre stage—the highlight of the show—and you get 90 thirty-second performances as each vehicle rolls onto the dock and drives up Chemin du Débarcadère. "Look how big that bus is! How can it fit in there? Look at all those bicycles on top of that van! Is that a gold Cadillac? I've never seen a Winnebago that long. Wow, a motorcycle gang with Harley Davidsons!" It's the best show in town—hands down!

The green building at the top of Chemin du Débarcadère—the Tourist Bureau—is suddenly swamped with cars and people searching for a room for the night, a nearby camp ground, or a recommendation for dinner. The Tourist Bureau (Association Touristique des Îles-de-la-Madeleine) is an unusually shaped structure with large poles at each corner. Its architecture represents the traditional Magdalen Islands hay barrack, which was used to store and shelter hay.

Left, right, left, and right again—one by one the cars turn onto Highway 199 and vanish. Within an hour the hustle and bustle of the ferry has died, soaked up by the islands. Tranquillity returns to the port—until tomorrow.

Château Madelinot

Seal Watching:

During winter, snow and ice transform the Magdalens into a magnificent lunar landscape. For a few months, land and sea are intertwined with a silvery white blanket that reflects the ever-changing light.

Every March, an unforgettable cycle repeats itself off the coast of the islands. Hundreds of thousands of Harp Seals migrate from Greenland to the Gulf of St. Lawrence to give birth to their pups.

It's one of the most moving and spectacular sights in North America, and it can be observed in relative ease and safety. And very few people have seen it.

Hundreds of thousands of Harp Seals migrate from the arctic waters of Greenland to give birth to seal pups just off the coast of the Magdalen Islands.

Within seconds of the distinctive sound of helicopter blades, you're high above the Château Madelinot headed towards the frozen Gulf of St. Lawrence—and the vast seal herd. Below is the endless expanse of the Great Barrier Ice Floe. The immense sheet is dotted with thousands of grey seals as far as the eye can see.

The pilot gently sets down on the ice, and you step out amidst hundreds of furry white balls wriggling along the ice. Approaching these wonderful creatures, you'll be captivated by their gentle and inquisitive eyes. You may catch a glimpse of rare Hooded Seals frolicking in open water.

The Château Madelinot is perhaps the largest adventure tour operator on the Magdalen Islands. They offer bird-watching,

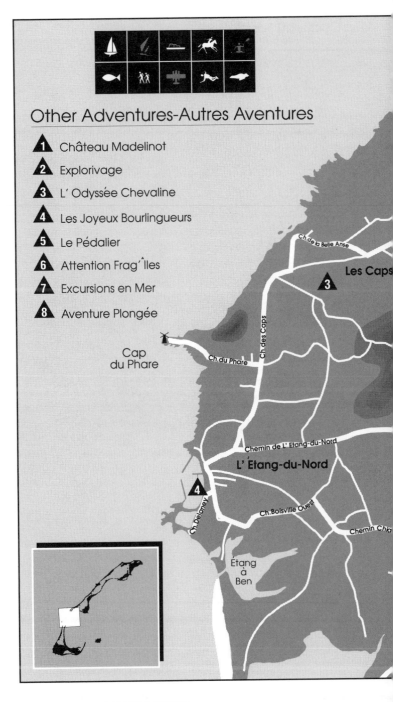

Other Adventures-Autres Aventures

1 Château Madelinot

2 Explorivage

3 L' Odyssée Chevaline

4 Les Joyeux Bourlingueurs

5 Le Pédalier

6 Attention Frag´ Îles

7 Excursions en Mer

8 Aventure Plongée

Ch.de la Belle Anse

Les Caps

3

Ch.des Caps

Cap
du Phare

Ch.du Phare

Chemin de L' Etang-du-Nord

L' Étang-du-Nord

4

Ch.Delaney

Ch.Boisville Ouest

Chemin Chia

Étang
à
Ben

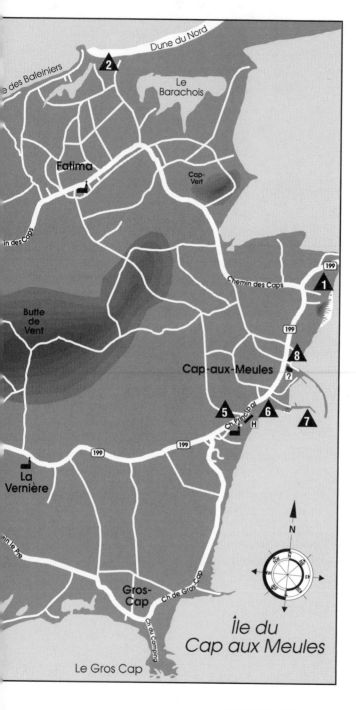

Dune du Nord

e des Baleiniers

Le
Barachois

Fatima

Cap-
Vert

in des Caps

Chemin des Caps

199

1

199

Butte
de
Vent

8

Cap-aux-Meules

?

5

6

7

Ch. Principal

H

199

199

La
Vernière

in le Pre

N

Gros-
Cap

Ch. de Gros-Cap

Île du
Cap aux Meules

Ch. du Camping

Le Gros Cap

horseback riding, scuba diving, deep-sea fishing, dogsledding, cross-country skiing, and helicopter adventures. And by the time this book is released, they'll probably have added a few more.

How to Get There:
From the Tourist Bureau, turn right on Chemin Principal following signs for 199 East. The Château Madelinot is approximately 3 km (1 mi.) and only a few minutes from the Tourist Bureau, on your right. You can't miss it—it's the largest hotel on the island.

For Further Information:
Château Madelinot, 323 Route Principal, P.O. Box 265, Cap-aux-Meules, Îles-de-la-Madeleine, Quebec, GOB 1BO. Tel: (418) 986-3695. Fax: (418) 986-6437.

Explorivage
Geological Interpretation Centre

Zodiac Guided Excursions:
Imagine gliding beneath towering cliffs in a zodiac, weaving in and out of mysterious caves, tunnels, and arches. How did these formations develop? Why are the cliffs so red? What type of rock are the cliffs made of? Why is this grotto called the Cathedral? You'll get the answers and learn much more about the fascinating geography of the islands by taking a guided excursion with Explorivage. They offer four exciting circuits that explore various geographical aspects of the islands.

How to Get There:
From the Tourist Bureau, turn right on Chemin Principal following signs for 199 East. At Chemin des Cap—which is across from the Château Madelinot, turn left and continue until you reach Chemin de L'Hôpital. Turn right on Chemin de L'Hôpital and continue to the Anse-aux-Baleiniers recreation centre. It's about 6 km (4 mi.)—a five-minute car ride—to the centre.

For Further Information:
Explorivage, Boite 4, Les Caps, Îles-de-la-Madeleine, Quebec, GOB 1GO. Tel: (418) 986-5005.

L'Odyssée Chevaline

What could be more thrilling than riding horseback along the cliffs at La Belle Anse—the wild foaming sea on the your left and a forest on your right? Well ... you could be trotting to the summit of La Butte du Vent—the second highest mountain on the Magdalen Islands—for a spectacular view of the archipelago, or you could be galloping along the deserted beaches of La Plage de la Dune du Nord. Exploring the islands from the saddle is a unique experience.

For Further Information and Directions:
L'Odyssée Chevaline, Centre Equestre, Chemin Les Caps, Fatima, (Dépanneur Chevarie). Tel: (418) 986-3177.

Les Joyeux Bourlingueurs

Legend of Le Corps Mort
There is an old saying about Le Corps Mort—that God created the land, and the devil tried to create something equally beautiful, but could only make this barren rock, enshrouded perpetually in fog. Le Corps Mort, or Dead Man's Island, sits about 10 km (6 mi.) off the western edge of Île du Havre Aubert. It resembles the shape of a dead man, arms folded across his breast. For centuries, it has wreaked havoc on sailors, but Captain Yvon Renaud promises a safe voyage aboard the *Joyeux Bourlingueurs*. You'll marvel at the hundreds of grey seals inhabiting the island's rocky pinnacles. You may even spot one of the shipwrecks strewn throughout the marine graveyard.

How to Get There:
From the Tourist Bureau, turn left on Chemin Principal following signs for 199 West. After passing the white wooden church at La Vernière, you'll see a sign for Havre-Aubert and L'Étang-du-Nord. Continue along Chemin de L'Étang-du-Nord to the port. It's about 8 km (5 mi.)—ten minutes by car.

For Further Information:
Les Joyeux Bourlingueurs, Captain Yvon Renaud, C.P. 1331, L'Étang-du-Nord, Îles-de-la-Madeleine, Quebec, GOB 1EO. Tel: (418) 986-3997.

Le Pédalier (The Pedaler)

Le Tour des Îles:
Going into its fourth season now, Le Tour des Îles is organized by André Therien and Bernard Bacon of Le Pédalier. The tour is a cycling race from one tip of the archipelago—Musée de la Mer (Havre-Aubert)—to the other (Grande-Entrée). Having completed the 88-km (55-mi.) race and received my Certificate of Merit—which hangs proudly in my office—I can genuinely say that it's a fantastic ride. My friend Arthur Miousse and I were cheered on by our wives and friends right to the finish line. The race is well organized and is a great way to experience the islands.

Besides bicycle rentals and repairs, Le Pédalier offers cycling tour packages that include accommodations, meals, and equipment.

How to Get There:
From the Tourist Bureau, turn left on Chemin Principal following signs for 199 West. Le Pédalier is at the corner of Chemin Principal and Chemin Petitpas on the right side of the road. (It's also the first traffic light.) It's about 2 km (1 mi.) from the Tourist Bureau—two minutes by car.

For Further Information:
To get the dates for Le Tour des Îles, or for a cycling package tour, or if you just need advice on routes, or some repairs, contact: Le Pédalier, 365 Chemin Principal, Cap-aux-Meules. Tel: (418) 986-2965.

Attention Frag'Îles

Nature Interpretation Hikes:
Attention Frag'Îles is a non-profit organization devoted to preserving the fragile ecological environment of the Magdalen Islands. It offers special conservation programs, education, and nature trails. If you want a guided hike with people who know the flora, fauna, and environmental issues of the islands, look no further. Throughout the summer, guides lead informative walks through the dunes and wetlands.

For further information:
Attention Frag'Îles, C.P. 369, Cap-aux-Meules, Îles-de-la-Madeleine, Quebec, G0B 1B0. Tel: (418) 986-6644/6633.

Excursions en Mer

Boat Excursions

Offers a close look at the famous Elephant, or sea voyages to Île d'Entrée or Rocher aux Oiseaux. Captain Gaston Arseneau—a seasoned skipper, who rides a huge motorcycle—is your passport to adventure aboard the *Pelican*. He knows everything about the archipelago, and his sea tales are spellbinding.

How to Get There:

From the Tourist Bureau, turn left on Chemin Principal. Turn left again onto Chemin du Quai and follow the signs for Excursions en Mer. It's about 1 km (.6mi.) from the Tourist Bureau—two minutes by car.

For further information:

(418) 986-4745/2304.

Aventure Plongée

Snorkelling at Gros-Cap:

(Reviewed by François La Roche)
"It was my first dive, and I was a little nervous about the 12°C (54°F) water. But the thorough safety briefing and the good humour of the guide calmed me and the others as we sat nervously in our seats in the Gros-Cap shower room.

We were told not to expect the Bahamas nor to expect to see a kaleidiscope of sea corals and multi-coloured tropical fish—after all this was the Gulf of St. Lawrence! What we did see, and what filled us with wonder and amazement, were the crabs, lobsters, different species of fish, and various algae along the rocky bottom. For three hours we bobbed in and out of caves and grottoes observing the fascinating

Observing the fascinating underwater world of the Magdalen Islands in scuba gear.

underwater world of the Îles-de-la-Madeleine through a mask and snorkel!"

How to Get There:
Aventure Plongée is on Chemin Principal, just across from the Tourist Bureau.

For further information:
Aventure Plongée des Îles-de-la-Madeleine, P.O. Box 577, Cap-aux-Meules, Tel: (418) 986-6475/4470.

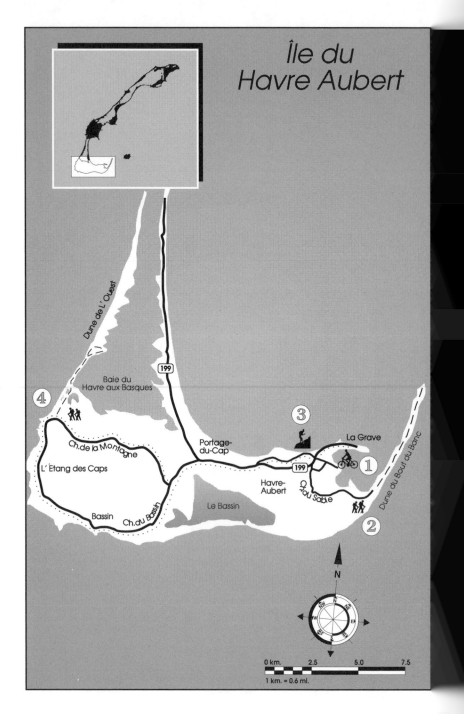

Île du
Havre Aubert

Dune de L'Ouest

199

Baie du
Havre aux Basques

④

Ch.de la Montagne

L´Étang des Caps

③

Portage-
du-Cap

La Grave

①

199

Havre-
Aubert

Ch.du Sable

Bassin   Ch.du Bassin

Le Bassin

②

Dune du Bout du Banc

N

N
NE
E
SE
S
SO
O
NO

0 km.   2.5   5.0   7.5

1 km. = 0.6 mi.

Havre Aubert

Route Length:
This cycling route is 37 km (23 mi.) long.

Approximate Time Required:
It'll take you from three and one-half to four hours to complete this ride.

Terrain:
For the most part it's fairly flat, but there's one very steep ascent—along Chemin de la Montagne—that's about 1 km (.62 mi.) long and climbs to about 100 m (328 ft.) at Butte à Isaac.

Road conditions:
Chemin d'En-haut, Chemin du Bassin, Chemin de l'Étang des Caps, and Chemin de la Montagne are well paved scenic country roads with light traffic. Highway 199 is the main road on the archipelago and can get quite busy relatively fast. On 199 be cautious, and stay well to the right-hand side of the road.

What to Wear/Bring:
Bathing suit for the Plage de l'Ouest, binoculars for Butte de la Croix, and plenty of cash for the exquisite artisan shops you'll see along the route—especially in La Grave!

Precautions:
Highway 199 is quite busy and drivers speed up there, so ride it cautiously. If you climb to Butte de la Croix stay back from the cliff edge—as always. La Grave is full of boutiques and artisan shops selling amazing things. It's very dangerous for your wallet!

Difficulty:
I love this ride for the varied landscape. One moment you're riding beside the sea, then around a bend you plunge into miles of forests. It's generally flat and poses little difficulty for most people. The long climb at Chemin de la Montagne is a bit tough, but you can walk your bicycle to the summit. Lots of people do!

Facilities:
There are lots of grocery stores and gas stations along the way, and they're indicated on the map.

Points of interest:
1) Artisan community of La Grave; 2) the Artisans du Sable sand-sculpture boutique; 3) panoramic views from Butte de la Croix; 4) traditional Hay Baraque; 5) lighthouse at L'Anse-à-la-Cabane; 6) port of Anse à la Cabane; 7) views of the island of Le Corps Mort; 8) islands off Plage de l'Ouest; 9) varied species of birds at L'Étang du Ouest.

Directions to Route Starting Point:
From the Tourist Bureau, turn left on Chemin Principal following signs for 199 West. After passing the white wooden church of La Vernière, you'll see a sign for Havre-Aubert and L'Étang-du-Nord. Turn left, heading towards Havre-Aubert. Follow the signs for Havre-Aubert and La Grave. Go through La Grave and up the hill to the large white building—Musée de la Mer. From the Tourist Bureau to here is about 28 km (17 mi.)—thirty minutes by car.

Route Description:
0.0 km (0.0 mi.)   Start out from the parking lot of Musée de la Mer.

The Musée de la Mer, on Cap Gridley, overlooks the port of Havre-Aubert and the tiny community of La Grave.

Before going anywhere, visit this delightful museum, which presents much of the history of the Magdalen Islands.

The maritime room uses black and white photographs, models, and exhibits to depict fishing, transport, navigation, and communication on the islands. There's also an exhibit devoted to shipwrecks. Out back there's even a cannon!

The environment room displays—through a glass window—the varied bird and animal life found on the Magdalens. The amphitheatre—La Muse—shows films and slide presentations on the life and history of Magdalen Islanders. It's well worth the stop because you'll leave here better informed about things you're going to see.

.3 km (.18 mi.)   Turn right out of the parking lot of the Musée de la Mer and go downhill on 199 East, passing through the community of La Grave.

The cluster of twenty or so grey shake-and-shingle buildings dotting both sides of the road are La Grave. The name comes from the French "grève," meaning pebbly and sandy terrain.

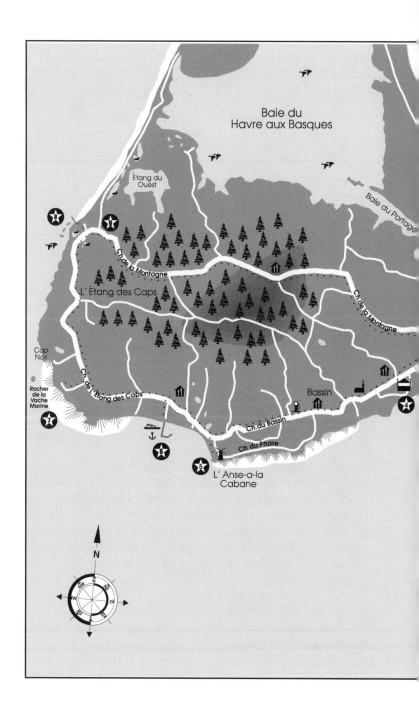

Baie du
Havre aux Basques

Étang du
Ouest

Baie du Portage

Ch de la Montagne

L'Étang des Caps

Ch. de la Montagne

Cap
Noir

Ch. de l'Étang des Caps

Rocher
de la
Vache
Marine

Bassin

Ch. du Bassin

Ch du Phare

L' Anse-a-la
Cabane

N

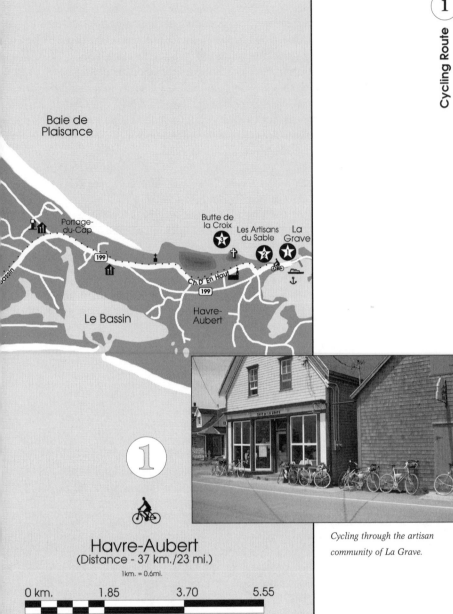

Baie de
Plaisance

Portage-
du-Cap

Butte de
la Croix

Les Artisans
du Sable

La
Grave

199

Ch.D' En Haut

199

Le Bassin

Havre-
Aubert

Havre-Aubert
(Distance - 37 km./23 mi.)

1km. = 0.6mi.

| 0 km. | 1.85 | 3.70 | 5.55 |

*Cycling through the artisan
community of La Grave.*

Officially designated a historical site on September 7, 1983, by the Quebec government, La Grave was the first fishing site on the Magdalens. Fishermen and merchants met there to do business. You can still buy dried and salted fish products in La Grave. Today, there's an artisan colony on this tiny spit of land that juts into the sea. Craft shops, cafés, restaurants, a bakery, an aquarium and a summer cultural centre and theatre—Au Vieux Treuil—line the narrow street. Rain or shine, you'll find cars, vans, and loads of tourists. Continue through the town, and do your browsing and buying on the way back.

.8 km (.49 mi.)   Just past La Grave, on your right, you'll see a sign for the Artisans du Sable (number 907). Stop!

Once you enter, the howling of wind and sea are transformed to the whimsical and melodic tinkling of chimes. You've entered a magical world of sand and sand castles. Vases, bowls, clocks, sculptures of a seal and a black whale, intricate sand castles, and lampshades all made out of sand—the unique expression of artists Nicole Grégoire, Albert Cummings, and Claude Bourque. "It is one of the loveliest artisan boutiques in the province of Quebec," visitors have said.

2.2 km (1.36 mi.)   From the Artisans du Sable turn right on 199 East, then right again at the top of the small hill onto Chemin d'En-haut. Stop just after the number 339 (on your right) to climb Butte de la Croix.

From the heights of Butte de la Croix and Collines de la Demoiselle you have a spectacular view of La Grave, the vast stretch of sandy beach (Dune du Bout du Banc), and the beautiful strand of La Martinique. For a more detailed description of the area and sites at Butte de la Croix read Climbing Route 3: Butte de la Croix on page 174 in Chapter 7.

2.6 km (1.61 mi.)   Continue right on Chemin d'En-haut, then turn left onto Chemin de la Baie.

3.6 km (2.23 mi.)   Turn right at the intersection of Chemin de la Baie and 199 East.

5.5 km (3.41 mi.)   Continue on 199 East until you reach Chemin du Bassin (there's an Esso station at the corner). Turn left

onto Chemin du Bassin.

8.7 km (5.39 mi.)   As you ride along Chemin du Bassin you'll pass La Baraque on your left.

La Baraque is a boutique in the shape of a traditional baraque—a structure with a sliding roof, used to shelter and dry hay. It's fast disappearing on the islands, but if you look carefully along this route you may spot one or two still in use. Inside the boutique you'll find alabaster sculptures by Daniel Renaud, as well as tiny wooden replicas of the baraque.

9.5 km (5.89 mi.)   Continue along Chemin du Bassin past the red-and-white church of St.-François-Xavier.

St.-François-Xavier-du-Bassin church has a mansard roof. This style of roof—named after F. Mansard, a seventeenth-century French architect—has two slopes on each of the four sides. The lower slopes are steeper than the upper. The two square towers were built in 1875. You'll see many homes in Havre Aubert with mansard roofs.

10.3 km (6.38 mi.)   Continue on Chemin du Bassin past the green house on your right—with a mansard roof.

12.3 km (7.62 mi.)   Turn left off Chemin du Bassin onto Chemin du Phare to visit the lighthouse at L'Anse-à-la-Cabane.

14.9 km (9.23 mi.)   Return to Chemin du Bassin and turn left. At Chemin de L'Anse-à-la-Cabane turn left again to see the Millerand Fishing Harbour.

16.9 km (10.47 mi.)   Return to Chemin du Bassin from the harbour. Turn left onto Chemin du Bassin, which now becomes Chemin de L'Étang des Caps. Turn left at the first dirt road at the top of the hill and stop in the parking area overlooking the sea.

As you face northwest, you should see off in the haze, an immense grey island jutting out of the sea. This island, about 10 km (6 mi.) away, is called Le Corps Mort, or Dead Man's Island. Shrouded in fog, uninhabited, and barren, this inhospitable rock was named for its resemblance to a human corpse lying on its back. The *Berwindlea* (1935), the *Beater* (1957), and the *Laura* (1868) are just a few of the many ships that have met their watery fate on its dangerous reefs.

20.6 km (12.77 mi.)   Turn left on Chemin de L'Étang des Caps and continue until Chemin de la Dune de l'Ouest. Turn left onto Chemin de la Dune de l'Ouest and stop.

The small ponds and lakes lining Chemin de la Dune de l'Ouest teem with birds—the Ruddy Duck, American Coot, Ring-necked Duck and many other species. This route cuts through two very different regions divided only by a sand dune barrier. On one side, the waves crash against the beach, on the other side, lagoons and marshes are eerily silent. For a more detailed description of Plage de l'Ouest, read Hiking Route 4: Plage de l'Ouest on page 178 in Chapter 7.

25.1 km (15.56 mi.)   Turn left back onto Chemin de la Montagne and continue upwards through the forest-lined route. The forest you're cycling through is the largest forest reserve on the archipelago.

29.9 km (18.53 mi.)   Turn left at the intersection onto Chemin du Bassin.

31.9 km (19.77 mi.)   Turn right at the intersection of Chemin du Bassin and Highway 199 following signs for Havre-Aubert and La Grave.

37.0 km (23.0 mi.)   Arrive back at La Grave.

You've finished your ride, and it's time for refreshments at the Café de la Grave. Once a general store, it's a wonderful bohemian-type café, just the place to unwind after cycling all day. High ceilings, one wall lined with books, the other with local artists' work, and the music of Edith Piaf. That should put you in the mood for some delicious home-cooked meals. A steaming potage, a croque-monsieur, or a slice of cheese cake washed down with a café au lait are all favourites of mine. Sometimes Jean-Marc Cormier plays the piano and sings. It's a treat all around!

Dune du Bout du Banc

Route Length:
This hike around the peninsula of Dune du Bout du Banc is 8.7 km (5.4 mi.) long.

Approximate Time Required:
It's one of the longer hikes in the book—about four hours.

Terrain:
Sand, sand, and more sand. If you walk on the foreshore—the hard-packed area near the water—you won't sink as much.

Difficulty:
It's quite a long hike, so you should be in fairly good shape. Hiking for four hours on a hot, sandy beach is quite demanding. My calves were aching for a whole day after I finished.

Precautions:
Protect yourself against sunburns and heat exhaustion by wearing sunscreen and drinking water regularly. The endangered Piping Plover nests along this shoreline. Its eggs are hard to see because they blend in with the sand. Watch where you're walking so as not to trample a nesting site. Avoid walking on the dunes themselves to protect the Marram Grass that grows there.

What to Wear/Bring:
Sunglasses, hat, sunscreen, plenty of water, high energy munchies, and a bathing suit are all essentials. I suggest bare feet.

When to Go:
A sunny day, and start out early—around 9:00 a.m.

Points of Interest:
Vast, deserted beaches—considered by some to be the most beautiful on the Magdalens. When you get to the tip of Dune du Bout du Banc you're within 4 km (2.5 mi.) of Île d'Entrée—an absolutely sensational sight!

Directions to Route Starting Point:
From the Tourist Bureau, turn left on Chemin Principal following

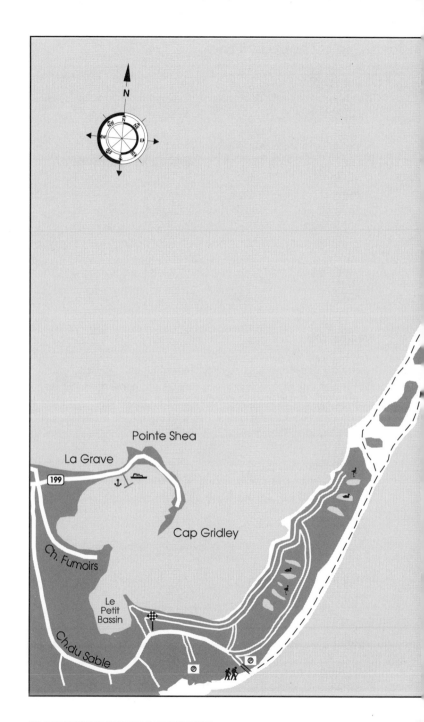

Dune du Bout du Banc
(Distance - 8.7 km./5.4 mi.)

1km. = 0.6mi.

| 0 km. | .53 | 1.06 | 1.59 |

*Vast stretches of deserted and
secluded beaches await at
Dune du Bout du Banc.*

signs for 199 West. Past the white wooden church at La Vernière, you'll see a sign for Havre-Aubert and L'Étang-du-Nord. Turn left, on Chemin de la Martinique (199 West) towards Havre-Aubert. Follow signs for Havre-Aubert. Turn right onto Chemin du Sable and follow signs for Plage du Havre-Aubert. The road eventually becomes a dirt road. At the black-and-yellow checkered sign, turn right. Pass the first parking area where there's a green sign— Plage de Randonnées. Stop at the second parking lot, on your right. From the Tourist Bureau to here's about 28 km (17 mi.)— twenty-five minutes by car.

Sand castle contest held in Havre-Aubert.

Route Description:

Originally, I was going to name this route Dune Sandy Hook— that's what maps of the island call this place. But when I was sitting at the Café de la Grave, talking with the owner, Jean-Marc Cormier, he convinced me that the locals know it by its proper name—Dune du Bout du Banc. Everyone in the place agreed with him, so who was I to argue.

Walk across the boardwalk onto the golden sand. Every August, the Concours des Châteaux de Sable, or Sand Castle Contest, is held at this spot. Started in 1987 by Albert Cummings and Nicole Grégoire, it's become one of the most popular events on the Magdalens. Amateur and "professional" sand castle

builders compete for the top prize of $500. The usually tranquil beach is transformed into a labyrinth of intricate, fanciful sand castles. The next morning, they've vanished—washed away by the tide—and the thousands of spectators are gone.

From this point, turn left, gaze across the seemingly endless stretch of white beach, and keep going for two hours. That's how long it takes to reach the tip of Dune du Bout du Banc.

As you walk, you'll hear the distinctive crunching sound of the sand underfoot. Gradually you'll edge closer to the water, the sand's firmer and the walking's easier.

Treasure hunting's the order of the day here. Broken lobster traps, Northern Moon Snail shells, razorshells, and delicate pieces of driftwood all invite scrutiny. It seems impossible to come away from a beach without a load of collectables.

Tracks in the sand are also irresistible. Are they Black-backed Gull, Great Blue Heron, Double-crested Cormorant, dog, or human tracks? Here's what I've learned. A Black-backed Gull's middle toe is straight, but it's other two toes are curved and it walks with it's feet turned slightly inward. The toes are connected by a web. Herons have three forward-pointing toes and one that points backwards. They have a long stride, so their tracks are often far apart. A cormorant foot has four toes pointing outward joined by a web of skin. All its toes are straight, and the front one is the longest. Cormorants have short legs, so their tracks are close together. I'm sure you know what dog and human tracks look like, but can you tell whether the person was walking or running? Walkers leave an even footprint, but a runner leaves a heavier toe imprint. That exhausts my knowledge of the subject.

When you pass the last sand dune you've reached land's end. The hordes of gulls and terns, used to having the place to themselves, wish you'd go away. At the tip, empty lobster shells, half eaten sting rays, and lobsters litter the beach—the remains of some birds' lunch.

It's a great place to rest and gaze at Île d'Entrée. Not many people come here, and after a while the birds just accept your presence.

On the way back I like to go skinny dipping in the warm waters of the lagoon. Don't forget to cross back to the east side of the beach at one of the openings in the dunes, otherwise you might get lost.

Butte de la Croix

Route Length:
This is another short one—only .8 km (.5 mi.).

Approximate Time Required:
It takes about twenty minutes to get to the summit of Collines de la Demoiselle and another fifteen minutes to get back down to the road.

Terrain:
The climb follows a double-track path that first twists up Butte de la Croix and then Collines de la Demoiselle. It's a fairly steep climb to the 82-m (270-ft.) summit.

Difficulty:
It's a pretty easy climb for almost everyone.

Precautions:
The cliffs, as usual, are very dangerous, so don't go close to the edge. It's also quite windy at the top—hang on to your hat!

What to Wear/Bring:
Binoculars, to view La Grave, La Martinique, and Île d'Entrée. A windbreaker might come in handy.

When to Go:
Any time.

Points of Interest:
From Butte de la Croix and Collines de la Demoiselle you have a spectacular view of the community of La Grave, the vast stretch of sandy beach—Dune du Bout du Banc—and the beautiful strand of La Martinique.

Directions to Route Starting Point:
From the Tourist Bureau, turn left on Chemin Principal following signs for 199 West. Past the white wooden church at La Vernière, you'll see a sign for Havre-Aubert and L'Étang-du-Nord. Turn left onto Chemin de la Martinique (199 West) towards Havre-Aubert. Follow the signs for Havre-Aubert. Turn left on Chemin

d'En-Haut and stop just past the house numbered 339. You'll see a white arch with the inscription "Jacques Cartier-1534."

Route Description:
From the road, follow the path under the white arch inscribed "Jacques Cartier-1534."

The route zigzags to the summit of Butte de la Croix, which you'll discover is a very windy place!

Facing east, you'll see La Grave—a cluster of grey-shingled traditional buildings dotting a delicate strip of land linked tenuously to the mainland. Its name comes from the French word "grève," meaning pebbly and sandy terrain. The oldest fishing centre on the Magdalens, it has been

officially designated a historical site. Fishermen met merchants here to sell dried and salted fish products—which you can still sample. Today, an artisan colony has sprung up along this tiny spit. La Musée de la Mer, the Aquarium, the Café de la Grave, Au Vieux Treuil, and many boutiques and restaurants line the narrow street. Rain or shine it's ususally swarming with cars, vans, and tourists. It's become one of the top tourist attractions on the Magdalens.

Butte de la Croix and Collines de la Demoiselle as seen from La Grave.

Behind La Grave are the sand dunes of the Dune du Bout du Banc (Sandy Hook)—a deserted beach that stretches for 5 km (3 mi.) towards Île d'Entrée where over two hundred anglophones live in relative isolation.

Retrace your steps down Butte de la Croix and follow the double-track road to the peak of Collines de la Demoiselle. Demoiselle means "young woman" in English, and these rounded hills reminded someone of the female form.

It's a bit steep but well worth the effort. From the summit, the northern half of the archipelago unfolds beneath you.

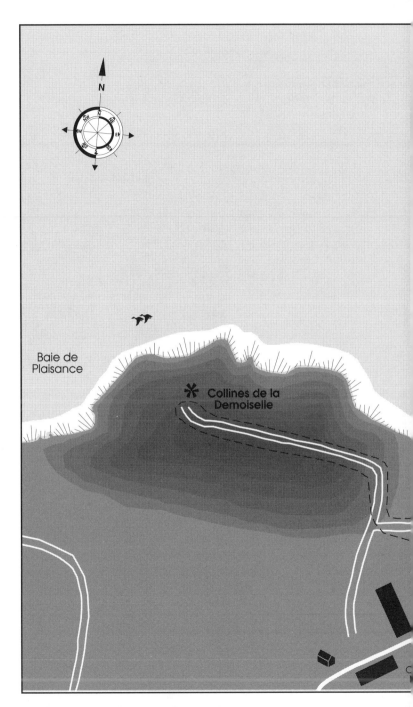

Baie de
Plaisance

Collines de la
Demoiselle

③

Butte de la Croix
(Distance - .8 km./.5 mi.)

1km. = 0.6mi.

0 km.   .07   .14   .21

Butte de
la Croix

Chemin d' en Haut

Garage
R.Bourgeois

urel
ert

Plage de l'Ouest

Route Length:
This hike is 2.85 km (1.75 mi.) long.

Approximate Time Required:
If you don't stop to go swimming—or to do whatever you wish—
it'll take an hour and a half.

Terrain:
Half the circuit follows a sandy road beside a marshy wetland.
Once you cross the dunes to the Plage de l'Ouest, you'll walk
along the beach.

Difficulty:
An easy hike.

Precautions:
Horseflies and dragonflies can sometimes be a nuisance on this
hike. The endangered Piping Plover nests in this area. Its eggs
blend with the sand and pebbles and can be easily trampled on.
Try to give them a wide berth. The Marram Grass—which helps
hold the dunes together—is also easily damaged. When crossing
the dunes, try to follow existing paths and avoid the grass. At the
end of the hike there's a dilapidated wharf. I'd stay off it.

What to Wear/Bring:
Binoculars—the birds expect to be looked at. Sunscreen and sunglasses are good sense.

When to Go:
Try the early morning. The birds seem more talkative then, and
their strange calls echoing over the silent ponds are hauntingly
beautiful.

Points of Interest:
The small pools and lakes along the route are full of birds. The
Ruddy Duck, American Coot, Ring-necked Duck, Common
Goldeneye, and Short-eared Owl are but a few. A field guide will
help you identify them. And don't forget to go to Plage de
l'Ouest. That's the beach of course—and it's a great one.

Directions to Route Starting Point:

From the Tourist Bureau, turn left on Chemin Principal following signs for 199 West. Past the white wooden church at La Vernière there's a sign for Havre-Aubert and L'Étang-du-Nord. Turn left onto Chemin de la Martinique (199 West) heading towards Havre-Aubert. After crossing the causeway, turn right at the Esso station onto Chemin du Bassin. Turn right again onto Chemin de la Montagne and stay on it to Chemin de la Dune de l'Ouest. It's about 32 km (20 mi.) from the Tourist Bureau—twenty-five minutes by car.

Route Description:

This hike goes through two distinct regions separated only by a sand dune that stretches for miles up the coast. On one side waves crash against the beach, on the other side, peaceful lagoons and marshes lie silent.

Follow Chemin de la Dune de l'Ouest north, passing a series of ponds and saltwater marshes on your right. These ponds are one of the best places on the Magdalens to observe waterfowl and other birds. Mergansers, coots, and grebes flock here to mate and rear their young. If you listen carefully, you can hear the delightful sounds that resonate over the tranquil lakes during mating season. Clucks, whistles, cackles, purrs, and quacks break the silence, reverberating from unseen places.

These very shy birds hide between the reeds and tall grasses, and dive quickly out of sight when spotted. If you're lucky, you might see a mother duck chasing four or five ducklings into the safety of the reeds.

Further along, Chemin de la Dune de l'Ouest narrows to a sandy path. On your right you'll pass the second largest lake on the islands—Étang du Ouest. The surrounding forest is one of the few mature forests of firs on the Magdalens. The island of Havre Aubert has the largest forest reserves on the archipelago.

Pass the pond with a small boat in it, then cross over the dunes onto the beach. Try not to trample the Marram Grass on the dunes. From atop a 9 m (30 ft.) hill of sand, you can see the spindlelike arms of Dune de l'Ouest stretching northwards to L'Étang-du-Nord and enclosing the lagoon—Baie du Havre aux Basques.

To the Northwest is Île aux Goélands, a tiny island inhabited by gulls, terns, and petrels. With binoculars you might detect the

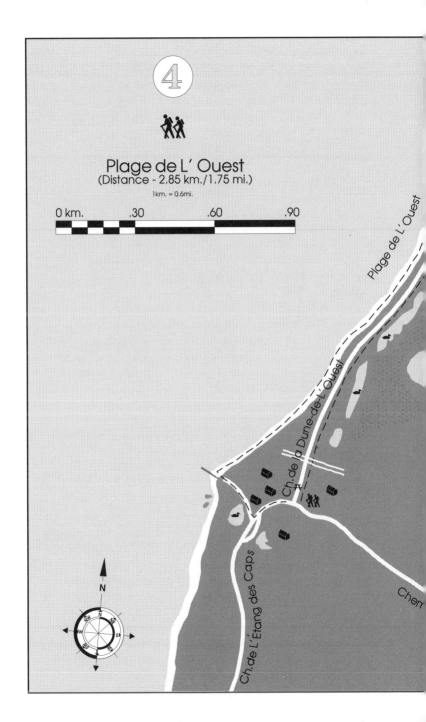

Plage de L' Ouest
(Distance - 2.85 km./1.75 mi.)

1km. = 0.6mi.

0 km.   .30   .60   .90

Plage de L' Ouest

Ch. de la Dune-de-L'Ouest

Ch.de L'Étang des Caps

Chen

N

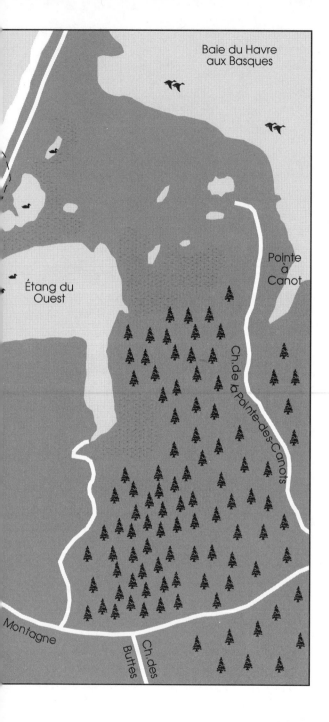

Baie du Havre
aux Basques

Pointe
à
Canot

Étang du
Ouest

Ch. de la Pointe-des-Canots

Montagne

Ch. des Buttes

A string of
fragile islands
on Plage de
l'Ouest.

remains of the *Corfu Island* further up the beach. On December 20, 1963, this Greek ship—belonging to Aristotle Onassis' fleet— sank in a violent storm. The last communication from the ship can still be seen in the Musée de la Mer, along with other arti- facts from the wreck.

Turn left on the beach and head south until you reach the remains of a pier.

As you approach the pier, you'll notice a group of tiny islands just off the coast. These islands were the cover shot for the beau- tiful photography book by Mia and Klaus *Les Îles-de-La-Madeleine*. About 10 km (6 mi.) due west from this point is the island of Le Corps Mort (Dead Man's Island). It's an inhospitable, barren rock which has caused many shipwrecks. Now it is home to hundreds of seals that bask on its shores.

On your way back, don't be surprised to encounter horseback riders galloping along the beach. The equestrian centre, La Chevauchée des Îles, opened in 1987 after importing five horses to the Magdalens. Riding along the beach at sunset has become a popular activity—and it's hard to imagine a more romantic one.

Turn left at the pier and follow the road back to your starting point.

Le Mamijo

Boat Excursions:
Captain Jean-Claude Poirier offers four excursions a day aboard *Le Mamijo*, out of the Havre-Aubert marina. Take a five-hour voyage to Île d'Entrée, sail alongside the cliff "carvings" at Le Gros Cap with a stop to see the seals at Cap Vert and dig for clams, or take a romantic sunset cruise in La Baie de Plaisance.

How to get There:
From the Tourist Bureau, turn left on Chemin Principal following signs for 199 West. After passing the white wooden church at La Vernière, you'll see a sign for Havre-Aubert and L'Étang-du-Nord. Turn left towards Havre-Aubert, following the signs for Havre-Aubert, then La Grave. Trips start from the marina in La Grave. From the Tourist Bureau to there is about 28 km (17 mi.)—thirty minutes by car.

For Further Information:
For reservations and information contact Captain Jean-Claude Poirier at (418) 937-5236/3223.

Centre Nautique de L'Istorlet

Nautical School:
The nautical school—L'Istorlet—is the biggest of its kind in Havre-Aubert and welcomes adults and children. It opened in 1973 beside the warm, protected waters of the Baie du Bassin—an ideal place to learn a new water sport.

If you've always yearned to sail, windsurf, snorkel, or use a kayak, you've come to the right place. Professionals will turn you into a pro before you know it.

How to Get to There:
From the Tourist Bureau turn left on Chemin Principal following signs for 199 West. Past the white wooden church at La Vernière, you'll see a sign for Havre-Aubert and L'Étang-du-Nord. Turn left, towards Havre-Aubert. At Chemin de L'Istorlet turn right and follow the road to the centre. It's about 23 km (14 mi.) from the Tourist Bureau—twenty-five mintues by car.

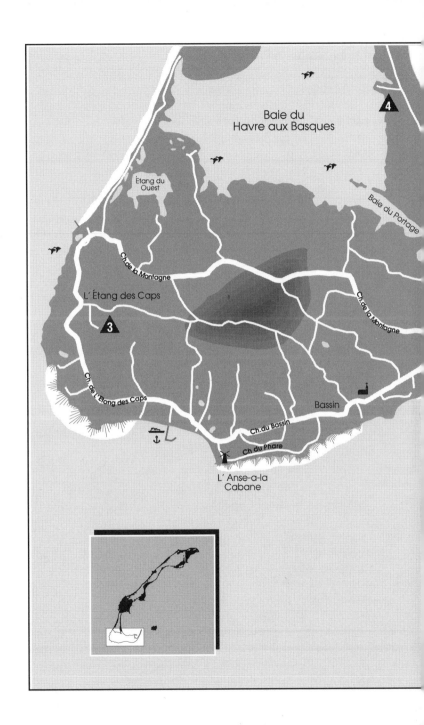

Baie du
Havre aux Basques

Étang du
Ouest

Baie du Portage

Ch. de la Montagne

L' Étang des Caps

Ch. de la Montagne

3

Ch. de L'Étang des Caps

Bassin

Ch. du Bassin

Ch. du Phare

L' Anse-a-la
Cabane

4

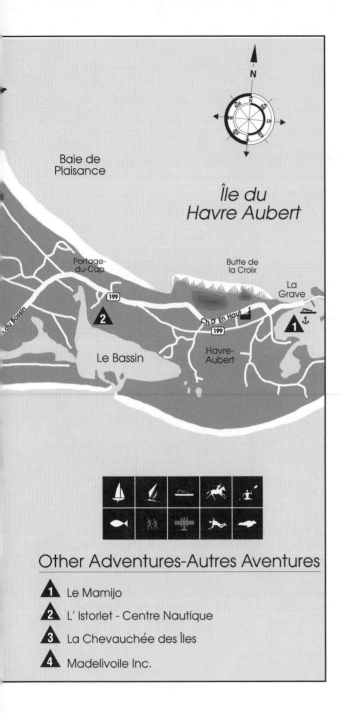

Other Adventures-Autres Aventures

1. Le Mamijo
2. L' Istorlet - Centre Nautique
3. La Chevauchée des Îles
4. Madelivoile Inc.

For further information:
Centre Nautique de L'Istorlet, C.P. 249 Havre-Aubert, Îles-de-la-Madeleine, Quebec, GOB 1JO. Tel: (418) 937-5266.

La Chevauchée des Îles

Horseback riding at sunset
on the beaches of Dune de L'Ouest:

(Reviewed by François La Roche and Gertrude Morin)
Galloping along deserted beaches at sunset—sounds like a dream, or a movie scene. You can do it in the Magdalens.

François La Roche and Gertrude Morin, honeymooners from Montréal, shared their feelings about this dream ride.

Galloping along the pristine beaches of Dune de l'Ouest at sunset.

"Horseback riding along the pristine beaches of Dune de L'Ouest was a once in a lifetime experience for us. It was exciting from start to finish, especially le Grand Galop—when the horses ran free and thundered down the coast, spraying sand and sea in all directions. As honeymooners, the feeling of riding a horse at sunset was a highlight for us—a memory that will last our whole lifetime."

How to Get to There:
From the Tourist Bureau, turn left on Chemin Principal following signs for 199 West. Pass the white wooden church at La Vernière,

and turn left at the sign for Havre-Aubert. After crossing the causeway turn right at the Esso station onto Chemin du Bassin, which becomes Chemin de L'Étang des Caps. At Chemin des Arpenteurs turn right and follow the signs for La Chevauchée des Îles. It's about 30 km (18 mi.)—twenty-five minutes by car—from the Tourist Bureau.

For Further Information:
For reservations (which should be made three days in advance—it seems everyone wants to be in this dream) and information, contact: La Chevauchée des Îles, Chemin des Arpenteurs, L'Étang-des-Caps. Tel: (418) 937-2368.

Madelivoile Inc.

Windsurfing in Baie du Havre aux Basques:
Carefree, untouchable—soaring like a bird over the crest of the waves. That's the exhilaration of windsurfing at Baie du Havre aux Basques—the "in" place to windsurf. Constant breezes of 15 kmhr(9 mph) an hour in a vast warm lagoon make this a windsurfer's paradise.

For further information:
Madelivoile Inc., C.P. 89, L'Étang-du-Nord, Îles-de-la-Madeleine, Quebec, GOB 1EO. Tel: (418) 986-3907.

Constant breezes of 15 km/hr (9 mph) and a large, shallow, warm lagoon make Baie du Havre aux Basques a windsurfer's paradise.

Île d' Entrée

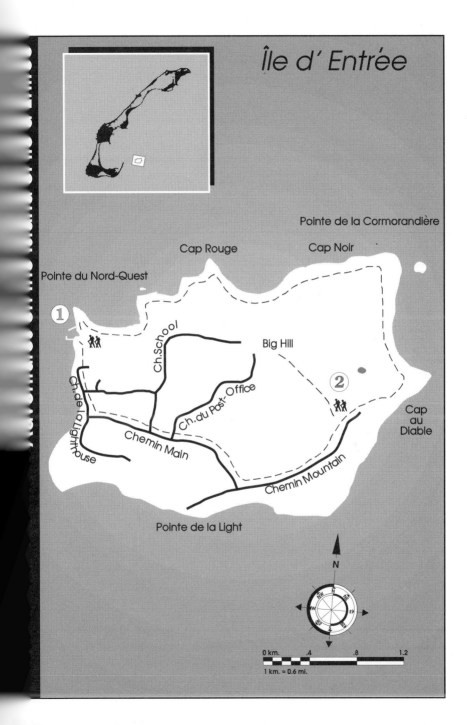

Pointe de la Cormorandière

Cap Rouge   Cap Noir

Pointe du Nord-Quest

①

Ch.School   Big Hill

②

Ch. de la Lighthouse   Ch. du Post- Office   Cap au Diable

Chemin Main

Chemin Mountain

Pointe de la Light

N

0 km.   .4   .8   1.2

1 km. = 0.6 mi.

Île d'Entrée

Route Length:
This circular route is 7.4 km (4.6 mi.) long.

Approximate Time Required:
The walk around the perimeter of Île d'Entrée takes about four hours—including a half-hour stop for a picnic lunch.

Terrain:
Along the northern cliffs, the trail usually follows a well-defined path through tall grass. You climb from 15 m (50 ft.) at Cap Rouge to 75 m (246 ft.) as you pass through a fence and enter the ravine near Anse du Nord, then to 90 m (295 ft.) as you approach the summit at Pointe de la Cormorandière. The terrain along the northern shore is a mix of tall and short grass. The southeast part of the hike, to Cap Au Diable, firsts dips into a valley near la Cormorandière, then rises to skirt around one of the largest hills—over 155 m (500 ft.) at the summit. This part of the hike also follows a rocky trail that's not always visible. This gives way to a double-track path through the grass, which eventually becomes a rocky dirt road that leads back to the harbour.

Difficulty:
You should be in good shape to take this long hike with several steep hills and long ascents.

Precautions:
The cliffs of Île d'Entrée are the highest and most sheer on the Magdalen Islands. Coupled with strong winds, they can be very dangerous. Be extremely cautious near the edge.

What to Wear/Bring:
I recommend plenty of high-energy trail mix, enough water, and a picnic lunch. Carry it in a back pack. There are no facilities until you get back to the town. Wear hiking boots, hat, and sunglasses.

When to Go:
Start early in the morning.

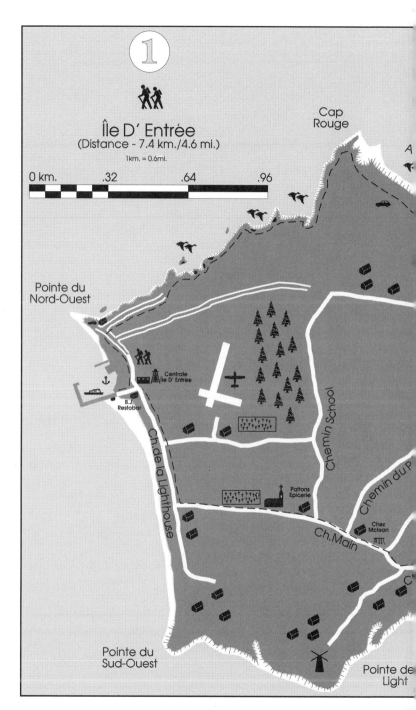

①

Île D' Entrée
(Distance - 7.4 km./4.6 mi.)
1km. = 0.6mi.

0 km.   .32   .64   .96

Cap
Rouge

Pointe du
Nord-Ouest

Centrale
Île D' Entrée

B.J.
Restobar

Ch. de la Lighthouse

Chemin School

Chemin du P

Pattons
Epicerie

Ch. Main

Chez
Mclean

Pointe du
Sud-Ouest

Pointe de
Light

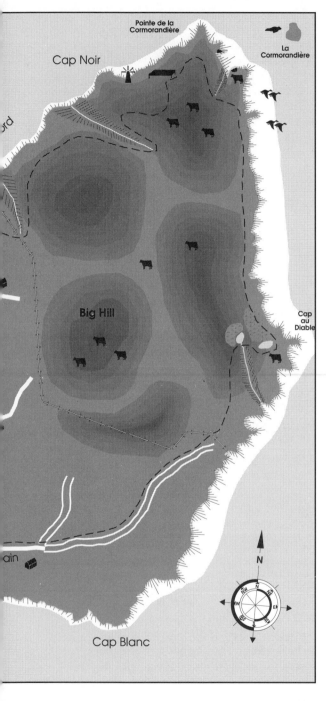

Pointe de la
Cormorandière

La
Cormorandière

Cap Noir

rd

Big Hill

Cap
au
Diable

N

ain

Cap Blanc

Points of Interest:

At Cap Rouge and Anse du Nord you'll gaze in awe at the countless Kittiwakes, Black-backed Gulls, Herring Gulls, and Black Guillemots crowded onto the face of the 50 m (164 ft.) cliffs. The rocky islet of La Cormorandière—off Pointe de la Cormorandière—is often host to frolicking seals. From the heights of Cap au Diable, on a clear day, the mountains of Cape Breton's Cabot Trail are visible to the naked eye. Hiking around Île d'Entrée is an experience like no other. Vaulting precipices and vibrant green hills seem to touch a deep blue sky. The air smells sweet; carpets of daisies sway in the wind; the sea surges in all directions; horses roam free and wild. Île d'Entrée gives you a sense of freedom like you've reached the end of the earth.

How to get There:

From the Tourist Bureau, turn left on Chemin Principal. Turn left again on Chemin du Quai, and follow the signs for either Excursions en Mer or the ferryboat, *S.P. Bonaventure,* which docks in front of the Coastguard building. It's about 1 km (.6 mi.)

The sheer cliffs along the northern half of Île d'Entrée rise abruptly from the sea.

from the Tourist Bureau to the harbour—two minutes by car. The ferry leaves for Île d'Entrée at 8:00 a.m. and 3:00 p.m. and returns at 9:00 a.m. and 4:00 p.m. The crossing takes about an hour. Excursions en Mer goes to Île d'Entrée at 10:30 a.m. and returns at 2:30 p.m. The telephone number for Excursion en Mer is (418) 986-4745. The number for the *S.P. Bonaventure* ferry service is (418) 985-2148.

Route Description:

Gaston Arseneau—Captain of the *Pelican Blanc*—pushed the silver lever forward, then backwards, and then forward again, and with one turn of the wheel the gleaming white boat was slicing through the calm blue waters of La Marina, Club Nautique—heading to the open sea. Our destination—about one hour away—

was Île d'Entrée. Three towering green mountains, jagged red cliffs speckled with hundreds of white birds, and a peculiar assortment of houses scattered randomly over the lush green hills was my first impression of this isolated place. Since my first voyage to Île d'Entrée, I've returned often to explore.

From the dock, turn left at the B. J. (Brian and Josey) Restobar and follow the dirt road to the second set of car tracks. Turn right, pass a deserted white building, and continue towards the cliffs at Cap Rouge. On your left you'll be able to see a graveyard of rusted cars at Pointe du Nord-Ouest.

From the cutoff, the path becomes less distinct as it winds along the cliffs in the tall grass—but it's definitely there. Continuing along the northern coast, you'll see several small islands just offshore.

You'll first notice a lot of gulls on the wing, then you'll stumble upon a sight beyond imagination—thousands of birds crowding the ledges of Cap Rouge and Anse du Nord. Great Cormorants, Herring Gulls, Great Black-backed Gulls, Black-legged Kittiwakes, Razorbills, Black Guillemots—all courting, displaying, and screaming.

At first glance the birds look similar, but each gull species is quite distinct. The Black-legged Kittiwake has a sharply defined black wing tip; the Great Black-backed Gull has black wings and back, while the Razorbill is a crow-sized bird—which is black on top and white below. It can be confusing without binoculars and a field guide.

From Cap Rouge, the path heads inland and upwards, towards a fence with a gate. It's lined with silverweed, buttercups, irises, and many dancing black-and-yellow Swallowtail Butterflies.

Beyond the gate, the path flanks a ravine and descends, then skirts the edge of a second ravine. Once around the second ravine, it climbs abruptly and strenuously to the summit of Cap Noir. At the top, you'll see a large wooden platform to your left. That's the picnic site—and a spectacular one it is. Congratulations —you've made it this far!

From here, on a clear day, you can see the outline of the Cabot Trail on Cape Breton Island—about 70 km (45 mi.) to the southwest.

After lunch, continue southwards down the valley, past the ravine facing La Cormorandière. You might have to pass through herds of cows browsing unperturbed by your presence on these

slopes. If you see some bones along the path, don't worry—it's not someone who got lost, but a cow that lost its footing and fell off the cliff.

La Cormorandière occasionally has seals basking on its shores. You might see them with binoculars.

The path climbs again along the eastern slopes of the mountain before descending to a small lake near Cap au Diable. From Cap au Diable the route runs along another large pond, then passes above a ravine before arriving at a fence with a gate.

At this point you've come in contact with civilization again. You've reached Chemin Mountain, but there are no street signs—in fact, none of the roads are marked.

Civilization here is an anglophone community of Irish and Scottish descent. It's home to about forty-five families, or about two hundred people, in about seventy homes—the oldest dating back to 1879. Dickson, Patton, Quinn, Goodwin, Mclean, and Clark are the names of people you're likely to meet as you walk down Chemin Main. On your right is the only bed and breakfast on the island—Chez McLean. Former prime minister Pierre Elliot Trudeau visited Île d'Entrée in 1970, but I don't know whether he stayed there.

Just past Patton's Grocery, on your right, is a white Anglican church built in 1949 and dedicated to the soldiers of the Second World War. Inside, the beautiful stained glass windows are a memorial to five young islanders who died at sea in 1987. The cemetery beside the church dates back to 1906, while the cemetery beside the airport dates back to 1855.

Turn right on Chemin de la Lighthouse heading back to the harbour. On your left is the Entry Island Lighthouse built in 1874. An electric foghorn was installed here in 1971. This lighthouse is one of the first and most dramatic sights visitors see as they approach the Magdalens aboard the *Lucy Maud Montgomery.* Having crossed at least a hundred times, I remember the excitement on board as we sail up the narrow channel past the lighthouse. The boat almost tilts as everyone crams the right side of the deck, gazing out onto Île d'Entrée.

On your right, just before you get back to the harbour, is the miniscule airport of Île d'Entrée, built in 1974. Craig Quinn, who used to live here, operates a daily air service to the island in winter—when it's the only way to get off the island.

Big Hill

Route distance:
To the top of Big Hill and back is 5.76 km (3.57 mi.).

Approximate Time Required:
It takes about three hours to reach the peak and get back to the harbour. Remember—you've a ferry to catch!

Terrain:
From the harbour, the route is mainly the rocky road along Chemin de la Lighthouse, Chemin Main, and Chemin Mountain. Past the fence, the stone path leads to a small meadow from where you climb straight upwards on a very steep, grassy slope to the summit at 174 m (571 ft.).

Difficulty:
Climbing to the top of Big Hill is harder than it looks. If you're in good shape you'll do it without too much difficulty. For the rest of you— be prepared to pant, sweat, and catch your breath.

Precautions:
The cliffs of île d'Entrée are the highest and steepest on the Magdalen Islands. The winds are strong. That's a dangerous combination, so be very careful. Less dangerous, but unpleasant, are the cow patties splattered throughout the area. The cows themselves are harmless, but not everyone believes that, so you might want to give them some distance!

What to Wear/Bring:
High-energy trail mix, enough water, and a picnic lunch—all carried in a back pack. It's a long trek, with no facilities until you get back to the town. Wear hiking boots, hat, and sunglasses.

Big Hill,
Île d'Entrée.

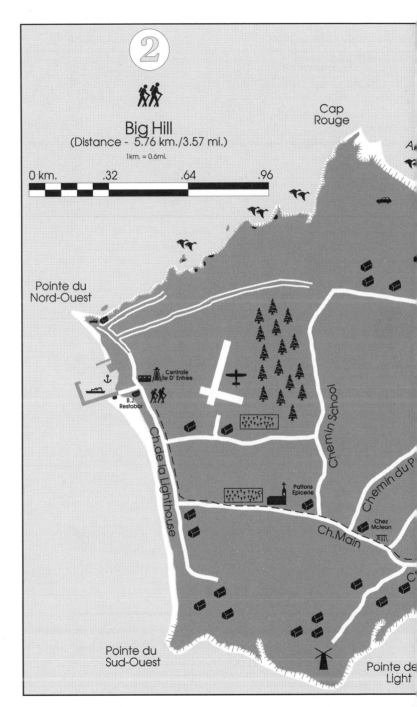

②

🚶🚶

Big Hill
(Distance - 5.76 km./3.57 mi.)
1km. = 0.6mi.

0 km.   .32   .64   .96

Cap
Rouge

Pointe du
Nord-Ouest

Centrale
Île D' Entrée

B.J.
Restobar

Ch. de la Lighthouse

Chemin School

Chemin du P

Pattons
Epicerie

Chez
Mclean

Ch. Main

Pointe du
Sud-Ouest

Pointe de
Light

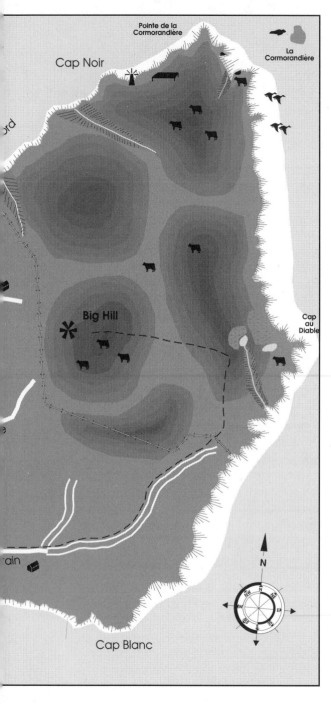

Pointe de la
Cormorandière

Cap Noir

La
Cormorandière

Big Hill

Cap
au
Diable

N

Cap Blanc

When to Go:
Start early—it's a long hike.

Points of Interest:
Why do people climb mountains? Wrong answer! The summit of Big Hill is the highest point on the Magdalen Islands. I won't even try to describe what you'll see. So the right answer's "because it's where it is."

Directions to Route Starting Point:
From the Tourist Bureau, turn left on Chemin Principal. Turn left again on Chemin du Quai and follow the signs for either Excursions en Mer or the ferryboat *S.P. Bonaventure,* which docks in front of the Coastguard building. From the Tourist Bureau to the harbour is about 1 km (.6 mi.)—two minutes by car. The ferry goes to Île d'Entrée at 8:00 a.m. and 3:00 p.m. and returns at 9:00 a.m. and 4:00 p.m. Excursions en Mer, leaves for Île d'Entrée at 10:30 a.m. and returns at 2:30 p.m. The telephone number for Excursion en Mer is (418) 986-4745. The number for the ferry service is (418) 985-2148.

Route Description:
The first thing you'll discover when you land is that although I've put street names on my map, there are no street signs.

So when I tell you to "Turn right on Chemin de la Lighthouse, left on Chemin Main, and continue straight on Chemin Mountain," what I really mean is, "Turn right on the dirt road past B. J. Restobar, turn left at the second intersection (which has the white church on it) and keep going straight past Patton's Grocery and Chez McLean B & B."

Eventually, the dirt road becomes a grassy path that leads to a gate in a fence. Past the fence, the path leads to a meadow and pond. From there the directions are easy—the climb's not. Find the highest point of land and keep walking until you get there. It's worth the climb!

For a further description of the sights you'll see along Chemin de la Lighthouse and Chemin Main, please refer to the Hiking Route 1 - Île d'Entrée on page 189.